A HANDBOOK FOR TEACHERS IN UNIVERSITIES & COLLEGES

A HANDBOOK FOR TEACHERS IN UNIVERSITIES & COLLEGES

A GUIDE TO IMPROVING TEACHING METHODS

Fourth edition

ROBERT CANNON & DAVID NEWBLE

KOGAN
PAGE

The reader may be interested to note that the authors of this book have set up a Web site – www.users.bigpond.com/handbook/ – which will help you to keep up to date and provides links to other sources of information and examples of good practice in learning and teaching.

First published in 1989

This fourth edition published in 2000

Kogan Page Limited
120 Pentonville Road
London N1 9JN
UK

Stylus Publishing Inc.
22883 Quicksilver Drive
Sterling VA 20166–2012
USA

© 1989, 1991, 1995, 2000 Robert Cannon and David Newble
Reprinted 1997, 1998

British Library Cataloguing in Publication Data
A CIP record for this book is available from the British Library.

ISBN 0 7494 3181 4

Typeset by Jean Cussons Typesetting, Diss, Norfolk
Printed and bound in Great Britain by Bell & Bain Ltd, Glasgow

Contents

Foreword

This is the fourth edition of a handbook that has already become well-known to many academic staff. Its popularity rests on the way it presents ideas about teaching and learning underpinned by research findings, but in a form that provides detailed, helpful advice for teachers in higher education.

Throughout, the authors consistently argue their view that the focus for teaching in higher education has to be the students, and the learning they achieve. This recurring theme means that the teaching recommended is student-orientated, yet it maintains the traditional aims of university teaching at its heart.

Too often, books providing advice for university and college teachers have a weak rationale, relying solely on anecdote and personal experience of teaching, and providing 'tips' without any substantial basis or justification. That approach often leads to inappropriate methods being used. Teachers in higher education have to be able to choose or adapt approaches to suit their particular subject area and students. Other texts on teaching and learning draw on dubiously relevant research findings and then become dogmatic about procedures, which, in reality, should always take into account the important differences in style in the ways people prefer to teach. In contrast, this book manages to ground its advice soundly in relevant research findings, whilst also drawing on a wealth of teaching experience to ensure that suggestions are realistic.

Clearly, the *Handbook* could be used to support any of the many training programmes being introduced into colleges and universities around the world, as indeed previous editions have already done. The various chapters focus on the specific skills that are dealt with in such programmes: large-group and small-group teaching, methods of assessment and so on. They also include advice on how to present conference papers, an area where advice seems sorely lacking.

The information provided throughout the *Handbook* is sufficiently detailed to guide the beginner lecturer step-by-step, whilst also describing interesting alternatives for those with more experience. There is a particular need for all staff to try new ways of organizing and presenting material for large-group teaching. The authors avoid the term 'lecture' because it brings to mind a didactic style of presenting information, whereas there are now many interesting ways to maintain both interest and engagement when teaching large groups.

This edition breaks with the structure of previous ones by introducing at the start a discussion of how students learn. This strategy ensures that readers realize why the 'information transmission' mode of teaching in higher education is no longer considered appropriate. Effective learning occurs when students become 'engaged', are active in thinking about the material being presented and intend to understand it for themselves. This means more than just through attending a lecture and so 'covering' the syllabus.

The research on student learning has introduced the idea of three contrasting approaches to learning and studying: 'deep', 'surface' and 'strategic'. While these categories inevitably oversimplify the complex processes involved, the distinction between deep and surface has proved very powerful in influencing the ways in which staff think about teaching (Entwistle, 1998). The research evidence now convincingly demonstrates how students' attitudes and motives, as well as their prior knowledge, affect the approach they adopt. It also shows how the students' approaches to learning and studying are influenced by the learning environment (the teaching, learning materials and assessment) they experience. As the authors of the

Handbook emphasize, there is thus a joint responsibility for high-quality learning. The students have to be prepared to work hard and develop the necessary study skills and habits, whilst the staff should create an environment designed to support the types of learning they believe to be important.

John Biggs (1999) has recently introduced the idea of 'constructive alignment', which stresses the importance of setting aims that recognize the primacy of personal understanding. These aims reflect the current attention given by 'constructivist' theories in educational psychology to how individuals construct their own understandings from information and ideas they encounter. 'Alignment' is necessary within educational programmes to ensure that teaching, learning materials and assessment procedures are all designed to promote and reward the deep approach. If even one of these components is out of kilter, then students all too readily drift into the surface approaches of routine memorizing and simply reproducing, 'parrot-fashion', the information presented by the teachers.

This handbook starts from these premises, and justifies their importance. But it then provides detailed advice and suggestions to allow colleagues to translate these ideas into effective practice. The authors draw extensively on their own teaching experience to make their advice both relevant and realistic. All in all, this new edition of the Handbook is very welcome. It provides detailed information about both traditional and innovatory techniques, and contains many valuable ideas about how to make teaching both more enjoyable (for staff and students alike) and more effective. It stimulates critical reflection on teaching and learning and, above all, it is enjoyable to read.

Noel Entwistle
Bell Professor of Education, University of Edinburgh
Editor of the international journal,
Higher Education, *(1993–98)*

References

Biggs, J B (1999) *Teaching for Quality Learning at University*, Open University Press, Buckingham.

Entwistle, N J (1998) 'Improving Teaching Through Research on Student Learning', in J J F Forest (Ed.), *University Teaching: International perspectives*, Garland, New York.

Preface to the Fourth Edition

Strong sales attest to the continuing need for a book on university teaching that is both practical and easy to read. We have been delighted on several occasions to find the book in use in many countries, particularly where English is not the first language. This suggests that our philosophy of easy accessibility is appreciated.

Preparing a Fourth Edition has presented us with numerous challenges. Clearly, much has changed in the years that have elapsed since we began to prepare the Third Edition in 1995. The growth in the use of the Internet and other electronic technologies for teaching, particularly in western countries, has been profound and raises many important questions. The pressure on institutions to cut costs and teach 'more efficiently' has intensified in a move towards greater accountability. In more universities than ever before, participation in some form of programme designed to 'teach teachers how to teach' is mandatory, and we know that our book has been used successfully as a basic text for these programmes. In this edition, we have attempted to face these changes and to address them in practical ways.

First, we have tackled the need to update the chapters and have incorporated new ones to cover recent developments.

Second, to ensure that we are in touch with the needs of readers, we have taken the opportunity to evaluate the strengths and weaknesses of the last edition and to take account of what we learnt from this.

Third, while we have preserved the very practical nature of the book and its contents, we feel that it is desirable to base our approach and the structure of the book very firmly on our current understanding of what contributes to effective learning in higher education. Therefore, readers will note a different ordering of chapters to that in earlier editions, with primacy accorded to student learning and to approaches that are likely to enhance the quality of their learning.

Our philosophy when writing this book has been to produce something helpful for busy university and college teachers that is both practical and easy to read. It is not intended to be a fully referenced textbook. This philosophy has underpinned each of the previous editions. Sales and the publisher's request for a new edition indicate the success of this philosophy and we maintain it in this edition. Equally, however, we recognize that there has been a considerable amount of research and development in higher education over the last two decades, and that the level of understanding and valuing of educational processes in higher education institutions has both widened and deepened throughout the world.

In response to these significant changes, we thought it was important for us to briefly present some key findings from this research and to set down some of our own values which have informed our construction and presentation of this book. The presentation, we hope, may also stimulate you to think through your own position with respect to these findings and values, and to develop your own teaching practices based on them.

In their landmark study, synthesizing more than 20 years of empirical research about how students change and benefit from attending university, Pascarella and Terenzini identify two persistent themes in the research literature, which we think are worth quoting for you in full here:

> The first is the central role of other people in the student's life, whether students or faculty, and the character of the learning environments they create and the nature and strength of the stimulation their interactions provide for

learning and change of all kinds. The second theme is the potency of student's effort and involvement in the academic and non-academic systems of the institutions they attend. The greater the effort and personal investment a student makes, the greater the likelihood of educational and personal returns on that investment across the spectrum of college outcomes.

These findings suggest something of a two-way bargain – a responsibility for teachers to build a stimulating learning environment based on interaction between teachers and students and among students, and a responsibility for students to participate actively in both the academic and non-academic life of the institution. These are themes that we will develop and provide ideas about how they may be implemented.

However, the research has produced more specific criteria of good learning and teaching that take these high-level generalizations to a more 'operational' level. These more specific criteria provide us with guidance in our work as teachers, and we have taken opportunities to illustrate them in this book. We find that it is useful to consider these criteria under the general headings listed below.

Relationships

The way in which you relate to your students and the way in which you help them relate to each other are vitally important. It is clear that a narrow concern for subject content or teaching methods and techniques (such as a fascination with the use of communication technologies) to the exclusion of a genuine consideration of students from all kinds of backgrounds is a barren course to follow. Genuine interest in students and their work, availability, enthusiasm for the subject taught, willingness to give helpful feedback, and a good sense of humour are all qualities that are identified as characteristics of the effective teacher.

Organization

Clear goals, course structures, careful planning, preparation, and clearly set out expectations and timelines are essential concepts in the teacher's organization and management of a programme of study. Students will be seeking clarity and systematic organization in the way teaching is arranged and managed at both the course and class level. One critical aspect of organization is the 'alignment' between the goals, the learning and teaching activities, and the assessment tasks that we set our students.

Instruction

This characteristic describes those teaching skills and abilities such as clear explanation, discussion, the use of materials, the stimulation of thinking and the strategies used to arouse the enthusiastic and active involvement of students in their own learning.

Assessment of student learning and the evaluation of teaching

This characteristic is closely related to instruction. Using assessment as a tool for learning and giving regular and helpful feedback on students' work are distinguishing characteristics of good teaching. So too is evaluation; this implies learning from students about the effects of your teaching, their misunderstandings, their approaches to studying, and their perceptions of the course and what you do – and do not do – as a teacher.

Subject knowledge

Whilst not denying the great importance of skill and knowledge in your own field, it is necessary to counter an attitude shared among many of our colleagues that it is the *only* important characteristic of the effective teacher. It is equally important to be competent in the other factors as well.

Other important issues

Finally, there are other important themes that characterize much of contemporary higher education. Some of these are far from new in concept, but what is new is a genuine recognition of them and a desire to address them in constructive ways. We have attempted to address these in our writing in addition to illustrating the implications of the research described above. We also acknowledge that university teachers in many different and diverse cultures use our book. Accordingly, we have attempted to address, where appropriate, matters relating to:

- A **diverse student population** and a concern to ensure **equity** in the education provided for all students.
- Strategies to **internationalize** higher education. For the purposes of this book, internationalization is the way in which we enhance the international dimension of education by the experiences we provide for our students through the curriculum and through the learning activities we devise.
- A growing recognition in research and practice of the **emotional aspects of learning and teaching**. Some current research and writing is addressing the non-intellectual aspects of our work as teachers and identifying strategies that can improve outcomes based on an honest acceptance of the feelings and attitudes of teachers and students alike.
- **Lifelong learning.** This is the implementation of practices in order to foster learning throughout life. Foremost among these practices is recognition of the ways in which students learn, and then building on this recognition in the ways in which we plan and implement our teaching. An important outcome of a lifelong-learning approach is the willingness of the student to continue learning supported by the capacity to do so.
- Greater **flexibility in learning** and teaching modes and materials.
- **Technology** as a tool in learning in teaching, but not as an end in itself.

USING THIS BOOK

In writing this book we have tried to keep in mind the

needs of the busy teacher whose main concern is to get access to straightforward ideas on some of the fundamental issues in learning and teaching without having to work through a lot of theory and jargon.

We have planned the book so that you can go directly to the topic of immediate interest. However, with this edition we have adopted a more explicit rationale for the way that we have arranged the chapters.

We begin the book with an overview of how students learn and some ideas on how you might use the research on learning in your teaching. This is followed by a sequence of chapters that move from student-centred approaches to teaching towards more general matters such as curriculum planning and evaluation.

As a general guide, to get best use from the book we suggest that you should:

1. Select an idea or set of guidelines from the book that seem to meet your needs and interests.
2. Carefully think through the implications of using the idea with your students and adapt the idea to your circumstances. Do not follow our ideas and suggestions too rigidly or uncritically.
3. Write out a plan of how you will actually use the idea. For example, if you decide to try the *Evaluation Discussion* technique described in Chapter 3, write out your own plan of how you will structure your time with your students and what you will actually do or say at particular stages of the discussion process. An important part of any plan will be the way you introduce your students to the idea.
4. Implement the idea according to your plan.
5. Review the success (or otherwise) of the idea and your plan with your students.
6. Try the idea again, being careful to replan and to build on your learning from your first experience and your review.

7. Undertake some of the suggested reading around the idea you are working with.

Our experience is that you will find, as many others have found, that the material here is helpful and constructive and will lead to growth in your satisfaction with teaching, as well as improved learning outcomes for your students.

Where to read more about issues and approaches relating to the Statement

In this Statement, we have touched upon a number of important and complex issues. We hope that you may have been stimulated to read more about these, so we have listed a few 'key' references for you to get started.

The first source is the one from which we took the quotation about the themes in the research on teaching. This book is *How College Affects Students*, by Ernest Pascarella and Patrick Terenzini (Jossey-Bass, San Francisco, 1991). The quotation is from page 648. This is a useful reference source and we suggest that you borrow it from, or acquire it for, your institution's library rather than buying a personal copy.

On the principles of good teaching in higher education, we suggest John Biggs' book *Teaching for Quality Learning at University: What the student does* (SRHE and Open University Press, Buckingham, 1999) and Paul Ramsden's *Learning to Teach in Higher Education* (Routledge, 1992).

An excellent introduction to the important concept of lifelong learning that covers a very wide range of related teaching issues is the Third Edition of Chris Knapper's and Arthur Cropley's *Lifelong Learning in Higher Education* (Kogan Page, London, 2000).

ROBERT CANNON
DAVID NEWBLE
Adelaide, 2000

Preface to the Third Edition

The need for a further revision of the book attests to the continuing needs of academics in higher education institutions for assistance in fulfilling their teaching role. In this revision we have updated all chapters, with particular attention to identifying more recent references. We hope that this process has not interfered with our basic philosophy of producing a book which is easy to read and practically informative. It is not intended to be a fully referenced educational textbook.

DAVID NEWBLE
ROBERT CANNON
Adelaide, 1995

Preface to the First Edition

In 1983 we published a book entitled *A Handbook for Clinical Teachers*. We did so for two reasons. Firstly, because we recognized that medical students were being taught to a large extent by people who had undertaken little or no formal study in the field of education. Secondly, because few books had been written to aid the teacher wishing to gain a perspective on basic educational principles and how these might be applied to teaching. The Handbook received a very positive response and after several reprints a second edition was published in 1987.

Rather surprisingly, we found that the book was being read by teachers outside the medical faculty who told us that the same problems existed for them and that the medical examples and orientation did not prevent them using the information, materials and advice in their own field. However, we were aware that a book specifically on medical teaching must inevitably have limitations. We have, therefore, modified the book to suit a wider audience. In some cases this has involved straightforward editing. In other cases, certain sections and indeed whole chapters have been completely rewritten. Inevitably, when writing for a wide audience there is a problem of selecting helpful examples of teaching or learning concerns: what will appeal to a teacher of literature may not appeal to a teacher of engineering. We have therefore striven to select from different disciplines in our choice of examples but where we felt the medical examples from our earlier book were helpful and relevant they have been retained. We trust that readers from other disciplines will be able to interpret these examples for their own needs. In making these modifications, we hope we have retained the character which has been so successful in the earlier versions of the Handbook. We look forward to receiving as much feedback about this book as we did from the medical version.

Finally we would like to express appreciation to our secretarial staff, in particular Ermioni Mourtzios; to MTP Press, the publishers of the medical version of the Handbook; and to Kogan Page, particularly our editor Dolores Black, for their support of this new project.

DAVID NEWBLE
ROBERT CANNON
Adelaide, 1989

Chapter 1   Helping Students Learn

INTRODUCTION

In what is intended to be a very practical book, this chapter will appear to be rather more theoretical than others, but we include it without reservation. We do so for two very important reasons. First, because the research and thinking about learning are yielding insights which help us to construct practical advice on a much firmer foundation than previously. The second reason is because of the fundamental challenge it provides to the more traditional views and stereotypes that prevail about students and learning in higher education.

Teachers have been primarily interested in *what* and *how much* students learn, and elaborate assessment methods have been devised to measure these. But in the last quarter of the twentieth century, a considerable body of evidence accumulated which suggested that we need to become much more concerned with *how* our students learn and the contextual forces that shape their learning. We need to appreciate that some of our students are having difficulties with their studies that arise not just from their lack of application or psychosocial problems, but from the specific ways in which they study and learn. We must also appreciate that many of their difficulties are directly attributable to the assumptions we make about them and the way we teach, organize courses and conduct assessments.

HOW STUDENTS LEARN

Although there has been an enormous amount of research into learning over many years, no one has yet come up with a coherent set of principles that would adequately predict or explain how students learn in any particular context. There have been psychological studies, studies in the neurosciences, in cognitive science, evolutionary studies, anthropological studies, and even archaeological evidence about learning to name a few! The paper by Marchese, available on the Web, provides a fascinating, scholarly and entertaining introduction to all this intellectual effort.

But it was not until 1976 when a landmark study by two Swedish researchers, Marton and Saljo, shifted from the traditional research focus on teachers and teaching to what students actually think and do in real situations. They reported on the approaches students take to their learning. It seems that all students have distinctive **approaches to learning** that we now understand are influenced by many factors, as shown in Figure 1.1. The

FIGURE 1.1 A MODEL OF STUDENT LEARNING

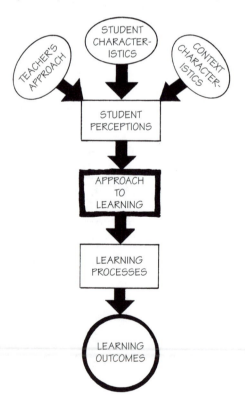

chain of events in learning and the links between them are the focus of much current research effort and so are likely to be refined over time. We attempt to summarize current understanding here.

One of the factors influencing learning is **student characteristics** and this includes individual differences, students' previous learning experiences and current understanding of the subject. Other influences can be grouped under **context characteristics**. This group includes the ethos of the department organizing the course and the characteristics of the curriculum. Closely related to this is the factor of the **teacher's approach** to teaching (a characteristic we discuss in more detail below).

The effect of these factors is to influence **students' perceptions** of their context and the **learning approach** that is expected of them. Students can be observed to use one of three broad approaches to learning, commonly called **surface**, **deep** and **strategic**.

Students adopting a **surface approach** to learning are predominantly motivated by a concern to complete the course or by a fear of failure. In fact, the emotional aspects of students' perceptions of their context is beginning to receive attention and it is emerging that anxiety, fear of failure and low self-esteem are associated with surface approaches. Surface-approach students intend to fulfil the assessment requirements of the course by using **learning processes** such as acquiring information, using mechanical memorization (which involves remembering information without understanding it), then reproducing it on demand in a test. The focus of this method is on the material or task and not on its meaning or purpose. The **learning outcome** is, at best, a memorization of factual information and perhaps a superficial level of understanding.

In contrast, students adopting a **deep approach** are motivated by an interest in the subject matter and a need

to make sense of things and to interpret knowledge. Their intention is to reach an understanding of the material. The process of achieving this varies between individual students and between students in different academic disciplines. The 'operation learner' relies upon a logical, step-by-step approach with a cautious acceptance of generalizations only when based on evidence. In such cases, there is an appropriate attention to factual and procedural detail which may include memorization for understanding. This process is most prevalent in science departments. On the other hand, the 'comprehension learner' uses a process in which the initial concern is for the broad outlines of ideas and their interconnections with previous knowledge. Such students make use of analogies and attempt to give the material personal meaning. This process is more evident in arts and social science departments. However, another process is that used by the so-called 'versatile learner', for whom the outcome is a deep level of understanding based on a knowledge of broad principles supported by a sound factual basis. Versatile learning does not preclude the use of memorization when the need arises, as it frequently does in science-based courses, but the students do so with a totally different intent from those using the surface approach.

Students demonstrating the **strategic approach** to learning may be seen to use processes similar to both the deep and surface learner. The fundamental difference lies in their motivation and intention. Such students are motivated by the need to achieve high marks and to compete with others. The outcome is a variable level of understanding that depends on what is required by the course and, particularly, the assessments.

The **learning outcomes** can be broadly described in terms of the quantity and quality of learning. The outcomes that we would hope for from a university or college education are very much those resulting from the deep approach. Disturbingly, the evidence we have suggests that these outcomes may not always be encouraged or achieved by students. Indeed, as we stress repeatedly, there is good reason to believe that many of our teaching approaches, curriculum structures and, particularly, our assessment methods, may be inhibiting the use of the deep approach and supporting and rewarding the use of surface approaches to learning.

NON-TRADITIONAL STUDENTS AND THEIR LEARNING

Institutions of higher education now enrol significant numbers of students (sometimes the majority!) who do not come directly from high school – what is often thought of as the 'traditional' source of students. Students from overseas and older students returning to study or entering without the usual prerequisites are just two examples of what we might call 'non-traditional students' in higher education.

There has been something of an explosion in the research and writing about these students and their learning. This literature is very revealing. In broad terms, it is showing us that any so-called 'problems' with these students is often the result of ill-informed attitudes and educational practices, in short, a result of poor teaching. This confirms the importance of creating a positive learning-environment rather than seeking fault with students.

Students from different cultural backgrounds

One thing we are sure you will have noticed in your institution or from your reading is that stereotypes are attached to students from different cultural backgrounds. One of these stereotypes is that students, particularly from 'Confucian heritage' cultures in Eastern and Southeast Asia, are rote learners. Yet many studies have shown that these students score at least as well and sometimes higher than western students on measures of deep learning. You may also have noticed how there seems to be a disproportionate number of these Asian students who receive academic distinctions and prizes.

The 'paradox' of these Asian learners – adopting surface approaches such as rote learning but demonstrating high achievement in their courses – has been the subject of much investigation. What is emerging is that researchers have assumed that memorization was equated with mechanical rote learning. But memorization is not a simple concept. It is intertwined with understanding, such as when you might rote learn a poem to assist in the processes of interpretation and understanding. Thus, the traditional Asian way of memorization can have different purposes. Sometimes it can be for mechanical rote learning, but it is also used to deepen and develop understanding. The paradox of these learners is solved when memorization is seen as an important part of the process leading to understanding.

We encourage you to read further about these issues, and about some of the other problematic cultural stereotypes (such as Asian student participation in classes) in the guided reading sources listed at the end of the chapter. They will not only help you to help these students become more effective learners but also provide a deeper understanding about the general processes of learning.

Older students

The literature in this area makes interesting reading. It tells us that older students are generally not much different to the traditional-entry younger students, and sometimes better in important ways. Figure 1.2 summarizes some of the key findings presented in Hartley's book.

FIGURE 1.2 *OLDER AND YOUNGER STUDENTS*

When compared with younger students, mature students:

● usually perform as well academically, and sometimes better;
● score better on measures of deep learning and time management;
● are generally similar on measures of ability;
● are no different in preference for instructional styles or in conceptions of what constitutes good teaching.

USING NEW TECHNOLOGY AND LEARNING

The literature in this field tends to be of two main kinds: that which has researched the impact of technologies such as computers on learning processes and outcomes, and the more general and speculative literature. Given the vast span of issues and time that this literature covers, and given the different methods used by researchers, it is difficult to draw from it too many useful generalizations to help you in your teaching, apart from the observations that:

● research on the impact of technologies such as computer-aided learning shows small, but nevertheless positive effects on learning and attitudes;
● studies on the impact of specific technologies (such as video and electronic mail) on learning show a great diversity of outcomes that reflect both the nature and the potential capability of the technology and, importantly, the way it is used by teachers and learners;
● the general literature is pointing to ways in which sensitively-used technology can contribute to a range of improved learning processes and to outcomes such as enhanced tools for learning, improved flexibility for those with access to the technology, individualized learning and more student activity.

If you are hoping to achieve spectacular learning outcomes by using the new technologies, you may be disappointed at this stage. However, we believe that there are opportunities to address many of the ills of education by using modern technology to support quality learning.

LEARNING MORE EFFECTIVELY

The concepts outlined above are not only supported by a growing body of research evidence, but also match the kinds of things good teachers know and do when teaching their students. We are in a better position now than we were in earlier editions of this book to make suggestions and offer practical advice based on the accumulating research evidence and the experiences of practising teachers in higher education.

Improving the learning environment

This must be considered at various levels. At the broadest level is the educational philosophy that underlies the whole curriculum. There may be little you can do about this, but there is evidence that students from traditional schools and teaching practices are more likely to adopt the surface approaches to a greater degree than students from programmes that are more student-centred. You may be able to gauge where the educational philosophy of your own discipline or curriculum fits and analyse the likely effect it has on your students' approach to learning.

At another level, and one where you might be able to exert some influence, is the structuring of the curriculum. You should be aware that the fragmentation of the curriculum into a large number of courses or course components taught by different teachers may be counter-productive to the development of deep approaches. The time available to each is limited, so the opportunities for students to come to grips with the deeper implications and perspectives of subject matter are similarly restricted.

In recent years, many different teaching methods have been developed, not from research studies, but from the practice and the experience of thoughtful teachers. In Chapter 2, Student-Centred Learning, we discuss some of these new methods. They are:

● problem-based learning;
● cooperative learning;
● students as consultants;
● service learning.

There are other methods that we could add to this list such as research projects, peer teaching, case method, learning portfolios, journals and more. Figure 1.3 lists the kinds of things that we can infer about student learning from these methods and the ideas that they have in common. The list suggests the kinds of things we might do, both in preparing the curriculum and in our day-to-day work with students.

FIGURE 1.3 WHAT CAN WE INFER ABOUT LEARNING FROM INNOVATIVE STUDENT-CENTRED METHODS? (Marchese)

Students are more likely to adopt a deeper approach to their learning and achieve quality learning outcomes when teachers provide for:

● intrinsic motivation and curiosity;
● student independence;
● student choice;
● opportunities to work with other people;
● an environment that is challenging, supportive and low threat;
● frequent, constructive and useable feedback;
● well-structured and clear organization;
● active involvement in realistic learning tasks;
● an emphasis on higher-level objectives;
● practice and reinforcement.

As most teachers reading this book will be working in a conventional institution, it is important to introduce these measures into courses that might encourage the use of the deep approach. Some other measures that you can implement are listed below:

- Ensure that the course objectives specify more than just facts and technical skills by giving suitable emphasis to higher-level intellectual skills, such as problem-solving and critical thinking, working collaboratively with others and exploring and developing appropriate attitudes.
- Introduce teaching activities that require students to demonstrate a deep understanding of the subject matter. Do not allow students to 'get away' with only reproducing factual information and take a genuine interest in what they say and do as indicators of their learning.
- Reduce the time allocated to didactic teaching to allow more time for students to work with other people and for self-directed learning.
- Decrease the amount of factual material that has to be memorized. Both the pressure of time and overloading a student with content are known to encourage the surface approach, even in those intending to use the deep approach. These problems are prevalent in many science-based courses.
- Spend more contact time helping students to understand and use basic principles and try to understand the difficulties they may be having (see Chapter 10, The Evaluation of Teaching and Learning, for ideas on ways to do this). Get into the habit of expecting students to explain answers to questions. The frequent use of the word 'why' will quickly establish if the answer is based on memorization or on the understanding of an underlying principle.
- Evaluate the extent to which students find you or their context threatening and take measures to eliminate or reduce this as much as you can, taking care to maintain acceptable levels of intellectual challenge.

● Most importantly, review the assessment procedures. This is a critical task. If the assessment, course content and learning methods do not match the course objectives, then you could be the world's greatest teacher and still make little impact on the students' learning. For example, an over-reliance on objective tests of low-level recall (true/false, multiple choice) will almost certainly encourage the use of surface strategies. If you aim to have students understand the subject, then you must introduce forms of assessment that require them to demonstrate their understanding. This may mean the reintroduction of essays, the use of research projects, self- and peer-assessment and so on.

Modifying teaching approaches

Evidence is amassing that there is a relationship between a **teacher's approach** to teaching and the quality of student-learning outcomes. Research and thinking about teaching over nearly 30 years shows that teachers hold different 'theories' of teaching and learning which influence their approach to teaching. Very broadly, there are teachers who believe their job is to cover the subject systematically by transmitting content to students. Failure to learn the content is seen to be the fault of the student. Teachers who have this approach to their teaching are more likely to encourage surface-learning approaches among their students.

Then there are teachers who consider the important aspect to be assisting student understanding and conceptual change. They focus on what the students do and what learning outcomes follow from their activity. This group considers failure to learn to be probably just as much a result of some systemic failure, possibly the way in which the curriculum was planned and implemented, as it is some kind of deficit in the students or their teachers. Teachers who describe their teaching as a student-focused approach are less likely to encourage surface-learning approaches among their students. We strongly suggest you read the article by Trigwell, Prosser and Waterhouse to deepen your understanding of these important relationships.

Teachers need to be aware of their approach and the impact that this may have on the **learning approach** of their students. We are not in a position to modify your beliefs and theories, although we hope that some of this information may help! We suggest that you experiment with several of the student-centred strategies described in this book and read widely – these will be important steps in developing a better appreciation of things you need to do to encourage high-quality student learning.

Improving learning skills

There seems little doubt that good learning and study skills contribute to academic success, though they are not in themselves a guarantee of success. Equally, possessing learning skills is now seen as having a lifelong relevance, not just limited to success in an end-of-course examination.

These lifelong-learning skills can be developed in your courses and include self-organizing skills; skill in deeper learning strategies such as analysis, judgement, synthesis and application; locating, retrieving, interpreting, evaluating and managing information; and the skills of breadth and depth of vision and the capacity to appreciate the interrelated nature of knowledge.

What is equally important is to develop your understanding of your students' conceptions of learning. If they believe that learning is memorizing information and reproducing it in a test (and this is what your tests actually reward!), then they will be likely to adopt surface approaches to their learning. Trying to get them to develop (say) group skills or skills of understanding or communication may be seen as a waste of time. Again, there needs to be a congruent match between your objectives, the way you arrange teaching and learning and the assessment.

For further information and help with specific study-skill counselling, we suggest you look through the vast collection of guides and manuals that are now available. These guides include valuable resources on writing and communication, matters that are of widespread interest to teachers and students alike. Choose carefully, basing your choice on your assessment of the guide's relevance to your discipline and the extent to which the guide facilitates the development of deep approaches to learning. Use the ideas in these books to inform your own teaching and suggest that students acquire one of the better books as a reference.

GUIDED READING

A very good general text on learning is *Learning and Studying: A research perspective* by James Hartley (Routledge, London, 1998). This is a particularly helpful reference for teachers as it simply and comprehensively discusses learning from a range of different research perspectives and makes practical suggestions on ways in which teachers can improve learning for their students. It contains sections that review the literature on older students and technologies discussed above.

Another useful source of research material is *Teaching and Learning in Higher Education* by Barry Dart and Gillian Boulton-Lewis (The Australian Council for Educational Research, Melbourne, 1998).

For an introduction to practical strategies and theoretical issues in lifelong learning, we recommend the third edition of Christopher Knapper and Arthur Cropley's *Lifelong Learning in Higher Education* (Kogan Page, London, 2000) and *Developing Lifelong Learning through Undergraduate Education* by Philip Candy, Gay Crebert and Jane O'Leary (Australian Government Publishing Service, Canberra, 1994). Both contain many exemplars of lifelong learning practices in higher education.

Recent editions (from around 1997) of the journal *Higher Education Research and Development* have published several helpful papers about Asian students. A particularly relevant edition is Volume 16, Number 1, April 1997, particularly the article 'Common misconceptions about students from South-East Asia studying in Australia' by Denise Chalmers and Simone Volet.

Strategies for teaching international students are discussed by John Biggs in 'Teaching across and within cultures: The issue of international students' in *Learning and Teaching in Higher Education: Advancing international perspectives*, edited by Rosalind Murray-Harvey and Halia Silins (Proceedings of the Higher Education Research and Development Society of Australasia Conference, Adelaide, July 1997).

For those readers who wish to read more about the research on Asian students, we suggest: *The Chinese Learner: Cultural, psychological, and contextual influences*, edited by David Watkins and John Biggs (Comparative Education Research Centre and The Australian Council for Educational Research, Hong Kong and Melbourne, 1996).

Guides and manuals to assist students with their learning skills, communication and writing include such titles as:

Allison, B *et al* (1996) *Research Skills for Students*, Kogan Page, London.

Hay, I, Bochner, D and Dungey, C (1997) *Making the Grade: A guide to successful communication and study*, Oxford University Press, Melbourne.

Hukin, T and Olsen, L (1991) *Technical Writing and Professional Communication*, McGraw-Hill, New York.

Books and articles referred to in this chapter:

Chambers, Ellie and Northedge, Andrew (1997) *The Arts Good Study Guide*, The Open University, Milton Keynes.

Marchese, Theodore, *The Adult Learner in Higher Education and the Workplace; The New Conversations about Learning*, available from http://www.newhorizons. org/lrnbus_marchese.html

Marton, F and Saljo, R (1976) 'I Outcomes and process', *British Journal of Educational Psychology*, **46**, pp 4–11. (On qualitative differences in learning.)

Northedge, Andrew *et al* (1997) *The Sciences Good Study Guide*, The Open University, Milton Keynes.

Trigwell, K, Prosser, M and Waterhouse, F (1999) 'Relations between teachers' approaches to teaching and students' approaches to learning', *Higher Education*, **37**, pp 57–70.

Chapter 2　Student-centred Learning

In the Preface and Statement of Educational Principles, we quoted from the work of Pascarella and Terenzini that summarized more than 20 years of empirical research about students at university. We reproduce that quotation again here because it explains the basis for student-centred learning. The authors report two persistent themes in the research:

> The first is the central role of other people in the student's life, whether students or faculty, and the character of the learning environments they create and the nature and strength of the stimulation their interactions provide for learning and change of all kinds. The second theme is the potency of student's effort and involvement in the academic and non-academic systems of the institutions they attend. The greater the effort and personal investment a student makes, the greater the likelihood of educational and personal returns on that investment across the spectrum of college outcomes.

As we suggested before, these findings indicate a responsibility on teachers to build a stimulating learning environment based on interaction, and a responsibility on students for active participation in that environment. Yet, if we look around, we find that much teaching and learning is designed and implemented in ways that achieve minimal interaction and which remove responsibility from students for many of the decisions and activities that could assist them to learn. In other words, they are not as fully *involved* as they could be in their own education.

Student-centred learning is a broad term that is used to describe ways of thinking about teaching and learning that emphasize student responsibility and activity in learning rather than *content* or what the *teachers* are doing. Essentially, student-centred learning has student responsibility and activity at its heart, in contrast to a strong emphasis on teacher-control and coverage of academic content found in much conventional, didactic teaching.

According to the recent studies we discussed in Chapter 1, teachers who believe their job is to cover the subject systematically by transmitting information to students are more likely to encourage surface learning approaches among their students. On the other hand, there are teachers who consider that what students do and the quality of learning outcomes that result from student activity is more important than subject coverage. Such teachers, who describe their teaching as student-focused, are less likely to encourage surface learning approaches among their students. We strongly suggest you read the article by Trigwell, Prosser and Waterhouse to deepen your understanding of these important relationships.

There are many possible distinctions between student-centred learning and conventional teaching and some of these are listed as examples in Figure 2.1:

FIGURE 2.1 DISTINCTIONS BETWEEN STUDENT-CENTRED LEARNING AND CONVENTIONAL TEACHING

Student-centred learning	Conventional teaching
students have responsible and active role (in planning their learning, interacting with teachers and other students, researching, assessing)	students often passive (no role in planning learning; sitting in lectures)
students required to make choices about what and how to learn	most decisions made by the teacher
emphasis on integrating learning across the curriculum	emphasis on learning this subject only
emphasis on enquiry-type activities	emphasis on receiving information
teacher as guide, mentor and facilitator of learning	teacher as expert dispenser of knowledge and controller of activities

intrinsic motivation (interest, curiosity, responsibility)	extrinsic motivation (grades, teacher praise)
focus on cooperative learning	individual learning and competition between students
learning can occur anywhere	learning confined to fixed teaching venues (lecture rooms, libraries, labs.)
greater flexibility in learning and teaching	relatively inflexible arrangements
greater flexibility in assessment with self and peer assessment becoming more common	assessment seen as the responsibility of the teacher with examinations as an important focus
long-term perspective: emphasis on lifelong learning	short-term perspective: emphasis on completing assigned work and learning for the examination

If we are committed to the goal of lifelong learning, that is, intentional, focused learning carried on throughout life, then moving to student-centred learning is an essential process to help achieve this goal.

Some approaches to student-centred learning can be successfully incorporated into the conventional curriculum, whereas others, when fully implemented, require a complete makeover of the way the curriculum is conceived and managed. A particular case in point is problem-based learning (PBL). Because of its growing significance as one the major innovations in higher education in recent years, we will devote much of this chapter to a discussion of PBL. We then want to introduce some other ways in which you may wish your teaching to become more 'student-centred' within a conventional approach. We would, of course, encourage you to experiment with these ideas and suggest that you read more and discuss your ideas with colleagues before you do so.

PROBLEM-BASED LEARNING

Problem-based learning has its origins in medicine and this is where much of its initial development occurred. Because this is the area with which we are most familiar, our examples to explain PBL will be taken from medical education. However, there have been many other disciplines that now use the approach such as engineering, social work, law, agriculture and management.

PBL is a way of designing and presenting courses that uses problems in professional practice or real life as the stimulus for student learning. Regrettably, many teachers immediately claim they have used this method for years because they incorrectly equate the problem-solving activities of their course with PBL. This kind of teaching is not PBL at all. PBL is a way of seeing the curriculum as being focused on key problems that arise in professional practice and which requires student activity – independently or in cooperative groups – to learn from the problems. Students work through the problems, under greater or lesser degrees of guidance from tutors, defining what they do not know and what they need to know in order to understand (not necessarily just to solve) the problem. The justification for this is firmly based in modern theories of learning which have found that knowledge is remembered and recalled more effectively if learning is based in the context in which it is going to be used in the future.

Thus, if basic knowledge is structured around representations of situations or cases likely to be encountered in professional practice in the future, it is more likely to be remembered. Problem-based learning is also integrative, with the need to understand relevant aspects of several different disciplines being readily apparent in each case that is presented.

IMPLEMENTING PROBLEM-BASED LEARNING

Problem-based learning will have different implications if you are involved on a curriculum committee than if your involvement is as a tutor to a group of students undertaking a PBL exercise. In the former situation, you will be engaged in reviewing the evidence for the effectiveness of PBL, in discussing the politics and practicalities of making such a major change to the curriculum, and in conducting or arranging information sessions and workshops for staff in order to gain their support.

Having decided in principle to proceed, your department may choose one of several implementation models (see Figure 2.2). You may decide to convert the whole curriculum to PBL or you may commence with two tracks, running the PBL track parallel to the conventional track with the advantage of gaining experience and undertaking comparative evaluation. If you wish to be more cautious, another alternative is to introduce PBL as a component of the curriculum or into individual courses with or without the expectation that the whole course will eventually change to PBL.

In any case, you should be aware that one of the most common sources of failure in PBL courses is to neglect the preparation of both other staff and students for this approach. Staff and students alike will need time and assistance to develop their understanding of the 'whys and hows' of PBL before they begin.

COURSE DESIGN CONSIDERATIONS

The basic principles of course design are similar to those in other courses. In general, PBL curricula are constructed in a modular format with blocks of several weeks being committed to a common theme. Factors to

FIGURE 2.2

IMPLEMENTATION MODELS

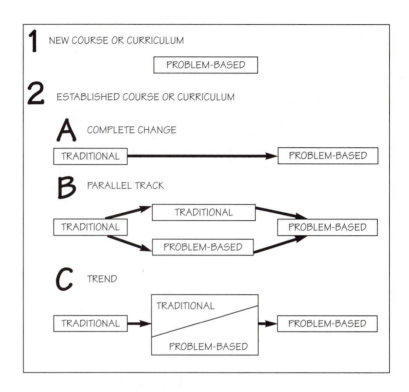

be taken into account are listed below.

The major purposes of the module

There are generally two major purposes to be achieved in a PBL module. One is the attainment of specific learning objectives in the form of an integrated knowledge and understanding of a defined problem. (As an example of a problem in this chapter, we will refer to an actual problem that we have used with medical students and with teachers in professional development workshops from disciplines other than medicine – a problem which almost everyone can identify with – diarrhoea!) The other major purpose to be achieved in a PBL module is skill in the process of problem solving and self-directed learning.

These purposes are combined in various proportions in the **Guided Discovery** and **Open Discovery** approaches. In the Guided Discovery approach, the emphasis is on both content and process. The course is carefully structured as a series of modules containing problems that direct students into learning the appropriate basic and professional content; for example, the basic and pre-clinical sciences and clinical content in medicine. While it is essential to allow students to discover the learning issues from the problem, written guidelines are provided and tutor prompting occurs to ensure that all content areas are considered.

The Open Discovery approach places more emphasis on the process. The framework of the course and the problems may be the same as the Guided Discovery approach, but the students have a much greater responsibility for determining what they should learn. Complete coverage of all content aspects is not expected.

The method of instruction

Problem-based learning is usually conducted in small groups of 5–10 students with a tutor. As a rule, the tutor is there to facilitate the process rather than to be a provider of content knowledge. In some schools, tutors are deliberately chosen to be non-experts, particularly where the Open Discovery approach is predominant. Small group activities are supported by the students carrying out independent studies, for which curriculum time must be carefully allotted. Where tutor resources are limited, it is possible to conduct PBL in large group settings, use student-led groups for discussion or rely to a greater degree on independent study. We have used this approach successfully in a foundation course on PBL for first-year medical students and we outline how it was done later in the chapter.

The selection of the problems

This is one of the most important considerations in course design. The problems must be of the kind that will be faced by the students after they graduate, but they must also be both broad enough and specific enough to engage the students in learning activities that match the curriculum objectives. Problems should not be answerable by simple responses. In general, they should be professional problems that will require students to go through the following process:

1. Analyse the problem.
2. Identify the knowledge required to understand and solve the problem.
3. Obtain agreement on the independent learning tasks to be performed.
4. Obtain agreement on when the learning tasks will have been achieved.
5. Apply the newly acquired knowledge to the initial problem.
6. Carry out further cycles of the process if necessary.

Preparing the problem-based learning modules

You may be asked to prepare one or more of the PBL modules. Your first task will be to obtain the objectives, or more likely develop them yourself. Such objectives should define what it is that the students should have achieved by the time they have completed the module. It is important at this stage to seek the involvement of teachers from all the disciplines that are expected to contribute to the learning outcome of the students.

Once objectives have been agreed, case summaries must be carefully prepared. Remember that they should be interesting and complex enough to engage students in the problem-solving process. A written guide should be developed for the tutors involved in the module; its content should depend to some extent on the degree of familiarity that the tutors are likely to have with the problem. An abbreviated example of such a guide is illustrated in Figure 2.3 for our diarrhoea problem. Resource materials for students and tutors should be identified (eg, references, Web links, audiovisual materials, computer simulations, static demonstrations and even lectures). Resource people who could be available for students to contact should be approached and times scheduled for meetings with students.

FIGURE 2.3 EXAMPLE OF A TUTOR GUIDE

PROBLEM – DIARRHOEA

Cases

1. Acute diarrhoea in someone who had recently returned from Southeast Asia
2. Chronic diarrhoea

Disciplinary aims

(a) Medicine/surgery

- Understanding of mechanism of intestinal motility; fluid and electrolyte balance in the GI tract; absorption (with applied physiology).
- Diagnostic approach relating clinical features to differential diagnosis.
- Investigation (clinical, laboratory, endoscopic, imaging).
- Management.

(b) Pathology

- Clinicopathological features of diverticular disease, bowel malignancy, inflammatory and infectious malabsorption syndromes.

(c) Microbiology and immunology

- Examination of stool for infective causes of diarrhoea.
- Clinicopathological features of infective and toxic diarrhoea (including traveller's diarrhoea).

- Role of gut in immunity.
- Immunizations.

(d) Clinical pharmacology

- Anti-inflammatory drugs in IBD.
- Antibiotics in infective diarrhoeas.
- Drugs for motility disorders.
- Supplements in malabsorption syndrome.

(e) Community medicine

- Control of community-acquired diarrhoeal disease.

References

- Standard texts.
- Journal articles (see separate list).
- Handouts (as provided).

Additional resources

- Pathology: demonstrations.
- Microbiology: demonstrations of GI organisms/ parasites.
- Self-assessment test.
- Radiology demonstration.
- Endoscopic pictures.
- Recommended Web-based materials.

ASSESSMENT

This is an area in which there is still considerable debate and development. As a start, it is as important to involve all the disciplines that are contributing to your PBL module in the preparation of assessment materials as it is to engage them in defining the objectives. Only in this way will participants be convinced that their discipline is being adequately represented.

Remembering that our concern is with student-centred learning, the most important focus for assessment in PBL is formative as it focuses upon learning. Constantly challenging the students to evaluate the success of their learning is a vital role of the tutor. In *Classroom Assessment Techniques*, Angelo and Cross present general strategies for formative assessment.

One way of planning assessment is to begin with the approach to PBL that you have adopted. In the Open Discovery approach, your assessment will tend to focus more on processes of learning, so you will likely use such methods as tutor-, peer- and self-ratings, and learning exercises which resemble the learning processes that would have been used in PBL.

Few assessment methods have been specifically designed for PBL. The best-known is the **Triple Jump Test**. As the name implies, this is a three-step procedure. In the first step, the student works through a theoretical problem on a one-to-one basis with a tutor. The student is asked to think aloud as the problem is assessed and learning needs determined. The second step consists of a fixed period of time (two to three hours) during which the student may seek out relevant information. The final step involves a return to the tutor where the new information is used to re-analyse the problem and to come to some conclusions. The tutor evaluates the efficiency and effectiveness of the student's problem-solving and self-directed learning skills. The outcomes are compared with the student's self-assessment of his or her performance. This method appears to have obvious validity, but as there is little formal information about its validity and reliability, its value for summative purposes has yet to be clearly established. However, do not let this deter you. In conventional courses where we *do* have quite negative information about the performance of some assessment methods, they are still used uncritically!

The Triple Jump Test can also be used to measure learning outcomes in the Guided Discovery approach.

Other methods that can be considered include simulations, essays, multiple-choice items which specifically and clearly target problem-solving situations (but never simple recall) and problem-oriented short-answer tests.

Students must also be challenged to develop self-assessment skills. A way of approaching this is outlined in Chapter 9 in the section on self-assessment.

Before embarking on the assessment arrangements for a PBL course, we suggest that you do two things. First, acquaint yourself with some of the literature on this topic (Part V: Student Assessment and Program Evaluation in *The Challenge of Problem Based Learning* by Boud and Feletti is a good start). Second, contact schools in your discipline using PBL to see what their current assessment strategies are and learn from their experiences.

TUTORING

A task which you are likely to have to perform in a PBL course is that of tutor. Your role will generally be that of facilitator rather than expert, a role you may initially find rather difficult. The sessions will usually be conducted in small groups, so Chapter 3 will also be helpful as a guide to the ways in which you might help your students to develop the necessary skills to work as effective group members. It is important to dwell on this matter briefly: if your students are to succeed in PBL, they must be assisted to develop an understanding of PBL and the necessary learning skills. These skills will be varied, but in most cases will include those of working in groups, information literacy (locating, retrieving and using information of all kinds), negotiating, interviewing and presenting. So, while you may not be teaching subject matter, you will have a vital role in helping them with the skills and processes of learning.

Modules are designed to be completed in a fixed period of time. For the purpose of this chapter the time allocated to a module will be assumed to be one week. A possible model of a week's activities is seen in Figure 2.4.

FIGURE 2.4
EXAMPLE OF WEEKLY ACTIVITIES IN A PBL COURSE

MONDAY	2.00–2.30	INTRODUCTION TO THE 'CASE(S) OF THE WEEK'
	2.30–3.15	'CONCEPTS' LECTURE ON MAIN TOPIC(S) OF THE WEEK
	3.45–4.30	GROUP MEETINGS (WITH TUTOR) – CLARIFICATION AND ALLOCATION OF CASE-BASED LEARNING TASKS
TUESDAY	2.00–5.00	AVAILABILITY OF DEMONSTRATIONS/ RESOURCE PEOPLE
WEDNESDAY	2.00	GROUP MEETINGS WITH OR WITHOUT TUTOR – CHECK ON PROGRESS – REFINE LEARNING TASKS
	4.00–5.00	CLINICO-PATHOLOGICAL CONFERENCE
THURSDAY	2.00–3.00	RECENT ADVANCES LECTURE
FRIDAY	2.00–3.30	GROUP MEETINGS (WITH TUTOR) – CHECK ON COMPLETION OF LEARNING TASKS AND PROBLEM SOLUTION – ASSESSMENT OF PROGRESS

At the first session, you will introduce the problem. Usually this will be a written case history (see Figure 2.5), but could be supported by a videotape of part of the history, or even by a visitor. Increasingly, the computer is being used to present the problem, often in very creative ways. One possible way of conducting this session is outlined in Figure 2.6.

FIGURE 2.5   EXAMPLE OF CASE-BASED PROBLEM

MR KIM JONES IS A 46-YEAR-OLD ACCOUNTANT. HE HAS RECENTLY BEEN ON A 6-WEEK TRIP TO SINGAPORE, THAILAND AND NEPAL. WHILE IN THAILAND HE HAD DIARRHOEA FOR TWO DAYS ABOUT THREE DAYS AFTER HIS ARRIVAL. THIS SETTLED DOWN WITHOUT ANY SPECIFIC TREATMENT AND HE CONTINUED ON WITH HIS JOURNEY TO NEPAL SEVERAL DAYS LATER. HE HAD NO FURTHER HEALTH PROBLEMS DURING THE REMAINDER OF THE TRIP.

HE NOW PRESENTS TO HIS DOCTOR TWO MONTHS AFTER RETURNING FROM ABROAD. HE IS CONCERNED BECAUSE THE DIARRHOEA RETURNED A MONTH AGO. HE SEEMS ALSO TO BE PASSING A LOT OF WIND AND THE STOOLS HAVE AN OFFENSIVE SMELL. HE IS OTHERWISE QUITE WELL.

FIGURE 2.6   PROCEDURE FOR INTRODUCTORY SESSION

Procedure (assuming students already have skills in working effectively in groups)

A Tutor explains that his/her role is primarily as a session facilitator, not as an expert on the content.

B Tutor ensures that everyone is introduced if this is a new group. 1:1 discussion is suggested for this purpose (see Chapter 3).

C Tutor provides students with the module handout which will include the problem case, list of resources, scheduled activities etc.

D Students analyse the problem case, identify learning issues and allocate learning tasks. Tutor ensures all expected outcomes are included.

E Students and tutor agree on future group meeting times.

Students are then engaged in formulating questions about the problem (eg, What might be the cause of the diarrhoea? Why did it resolve then recur? What was the mechanism for the diarrhoea? How should it be investigated?). To assist the process, you should be provided with instructions on the expected learning outcomes so that subtle guidance can be provided if the students do not identify all the relevant issues. You may also be provided with additional information about the case to feed into the discussion at the initial session or later on in the week. You should also have a list of resources relevant to the problem, such as articles, videotapes and experts available for consultation. There might even be a lecture or two for the students to attend. The expected level of tutor intervention will depend to some extent on whether the approach in your school is Guided or Open Discovery.

When agreement has been reached on the learning tasks to be performed, arrangements are made to meet again during the week to review progress and share information. You may or may not attend such meetings. Students will determine whether further information is needed and, if so, additional learning tasks will be assigned.

At the end of the week, progress with the problem is reviewed. Remaining difficulties are resolved. At such a time, some expertise relating to the problem may be of value. However, complete resolution of the problem is rarely possible, nor is it to be seen as the aim. Students should become aware that there is always more to be learnt.

If your institution is using expert tutors, it is unlikely that you will spend many sessions with one group of students. You may only operate as a tutor for a few weeks a year. On the other hand, if non-expert tutors are the policy, then you may be the facilitator to one group for an extended period of time. In many ways, this is likely to be more rewarding, albeit more time consuming.

STAFF RESOURCES FOR PROBLEM-BASED LEARNING

One of the major concerns for departments or schools contemplating a change to PBL is that of staff resources. It is widely perceived that PBL is dependent upon small groups and that this will require more staff, or a considerable extra time-commitment for existing staff. Where resources are an issue, it is possible for some educationally sound compromises to be made. For instance, if non-expert tutors are acceptable for some components of the course it may be possible to use staff who previously have not had a major teaching role and also some senior students as tutors.

Another alternative is to undertake the tutor-led sessions in large group settings as described in the next section. This approach requires skill on the part of the teacher. However, it is one we have found to be very successful and highly rewarding. Student feedback has been very supportive.

Of particular importance is the provision of staff training before embarking on PBL. Time spent on explaining the rationale and policies will be well rewarded as will a focus on the development of appropriate skills in tutoring and assessing in the PBL context. In our training we include the following topics and activities:

- principles of adult learning and the rationale for PBL, including research evidence;
- observation of an experienced PBL student group in action;
- participation in a PBL group, taking the roles of student and tutor;
- discussion of examples of cases, student guides, and tutor guides;
- group work focusing on the preparation of PBL materials.

PROBLEM-BASED LEARNING: CONCLUSION

By way of conclusion, we hope you can see how PBL is a fully developed and integrated approach to student-centred learning. The objectives focus on student learning processes and outcomes, learning occurs through individual and group activities and the assessment is aligned with both of these to continually steer students, with helpful feedback, towards planned outcomes and learning processes. There is a particular emphasis on formative assessment, or assessment for learning, rather than assessment to grade and sort students. In short, PBL reflects the key elements of the research finding introduced earlier in this chapter – the central role of other people (whether as tutors or as co-learners); the character of the learning environments they create; and the potency of students' efforts and involvement in the curriculum.

BECOMING MORE STUDENT-CENTRED IN YOUR TEACHING

Throughout this book, we have indicated strategies that you might use to move towards more student-centred and active approaches to learning. Examples may be found in our discussion of active learning strategies for large lectures and in almost all of our consideration of small groups. There are many ways in which you can become more student-centred in your teaching. Only your imagination and creativity in addressing the issues in your particular situation limit these ways. You may have already been stimulated to try some ideas that are part of PBL – such as the use of PBL in large lecture classes.

PBL IN LARGE LECTURE CLASSES

We have some experience of this derived from a first-year foundation course in which we aim to introduce medical students to the process of PBL. The main elements of our strategy are:

1. An introductory explanation of clinical problems (eg, diarrhoea in a traveller; chest pain in a squash player) is given to a whole class of 130–140 students in a lecture theatre session.
2. Students are asked to informally arrange themselves into groups of 4–5 to analyse the problem. The process of problem analysis produces a rewarding hum of activity in the lecture theatre.
3. The teacher then gathers together the ideas from this analytical exercise in an interactive manner from representatives of the groups.
4. Agreement is reached on the information that students require to proceed with the problem.
5. If the exercise is to be completed in one session, this can then be provided by the teacher or an invited colleague who is the 'expert'. On the other hand, the full process of PBL can be continued with students departing to report back at a subsequent session, having completed their independent learning tasks.

There are numerous ways that have been tried to move towards student-centred learning, some of which have a sound research base, while others are more experimental. We can only give the briefest detail and direct you to published literature for outlines of the theory, the research and ways to proceed.

Cooperative learning is one method that has received a lot of attention in the literature. This method provides a structured way of sharing responsibilities for learning in groups. A simple example is where the teacher assigns students to cooperative small groups in which they are expected to interact with each other, sharing ideas and resources, and supporting and encouraging each others' learning often by actively teaching each other and holding mutual accountability for achieving learning outcomes. We have found this to be a useful method where it is necessary for students to assimilate a lot of material in a short space of time, and where adequate learning resources (such as photocopied papers) can be provided. For a detailed review of this method and outlines of approaches, see *Cooperative Learning* by Johnson, Johnson and Smith.

Another approach to encourage student-centred learning is to focus on assessment arrangements, and here we refer you to Chapter 9 for a discussion on **self-assessment**.

What we have outlined so far in this chapter and elsewhere in the book are approaches that construct student-centred learning *within* the institution, although such approaches do not necessarily preclude links to the outside world (such as when students may visit experts in the context of PBL). But there are student-centred learning approaches that have an explicitly *external* focus. We shall give two examples of these here.

Students-as-consultants is an attempt to develop student-centred learning at the same time as linking education with the world of work. In this approach, students and staff offer free consultancy services to local businesses that involve work on real problems. The 'client' either gets a solution to its problem, or at the very least a perspective on it through fresh sets of eyes. Knapper and Cropley provide more detail on this approach, as they do on another closely related approach called 'service learning'.

Service learning is particularly prevalent in US universities and it relates students to their local communities as volunteers where they work with people, rather than with industries where they might ultimately find employment.

Service learning also has a strong presence in other countries such as Indonesia where it is a formal part of the curriculum. Not only do organizations and individuals in the community benefit from service learning as 'clients', but students gain valuable intellectual and attitudinal outcomes that broaden and deepen their academic work. Examples of service learning cited by Knapper and Cropley include educational psychology students working with retarded children; 'participatory action research' where students work on projects with the goal of bringing about change in the community; business students assisting local agencies with business planning; and English students working with community groups to edit and produce newsletters.

EVALUATING IN A STUDENT-CENTRED LEARNING COURSE

One of the challenges for evaluators in student-centred courses is to ensure that the evaluation methods do not distort the learning and teaching process in a similar way to inappropriate assessment of learning which can cause fatal distortions. A classic failure is to use evaluation instruments that gather data as if the course was *teacher*-centred, particularly the use of items that seek responses on teacher-presentation skills.

We suggest you refer to Chapter 10 on evaluation to review strategies that you can use to validly evaluate student-centred learning.

STUDENT-CENTRED LEARNING: CONCLUSION

We conclude where we started – with the research presented by Pascarella and Terenzini. Recall that they drew attention to 'the central role of other people in the student's life'. What we have seen here is a variety of ways

in which *people* are central to learning, be they other students, tutors, experts or members of the wider community. It may be that the connections made by students working with such people will be vital in the construction of professional and social networks in later life. It may also be worth thinking about the ways in which you could exploit the networking capabilities of information technologies to assist with this process.

Precisely defining student-centred learning and debating how much or how little of it to have in a course is much less important than the underlying values and approaches to learning that are involved and your intention to find ways to build components of 'student-centredness' into the courses for which you have responsibility.

GUIDED READING

There are many books and articles that provide the necessary background to the philosophy, justification and practice of student-centred learning and to PBL.

An important research-based text in this field is *What Matters in College?: Four critical years revisited* by Alexander Astin (Jossey-Bass, San Francisco, 1993).

For an introduction to some of the broad practical and theoretical issues in student-centred learning, we recommend *Lifelong Learning in Higher Education* by Christopher Knapper and Arthur Cropley (Third Edition, Kogan Page, London, 2000) and *Developing Lifelong Learning through Undergraduate Education* by Philip Candy, Gay Crebert and Jane O'Leary (Australian Government Publishing Service, Canberra, 1994).

An essential reference to have beside you with examples of PBL from many professions and with approaches to specific issues such as design and assessment is the Second Edition of *The Challenge of Problem Based Learning* edited by D Boud and G Feletti (Kogan Page, London, 1997).

Some of the seminal work in PBL has been conducted by Barrows, and two of his books are recommended. These are *Problem-Based Learning: An approach to medical education* by H S Barrows and R H Tamblyn (Springer, New York, 1980) and *How to Design a Problem-Based Curriculum for Preclinical Years* by H S Barrows (Springer, New York, 1985).

Books and articles referred to in this chapter

Angelo, T A and Cross, K P (1993) *Classroom Assessment Techniques, A handbook for college teachers*, Jossey Bass, San Francisco.

Johnson, D W, Johnson, R T and Smith, K A (1991) *Cooperative Learning: Increasing college faculty productivity*, ASHE-ERIC Higher Education Report No. 4, Washington, DC.

Pascarella, Ernest and Terenzini, Patrick (1991) *How College Affects Students*, Jossey-Bass, San Francisco.

Trigwell, K, Prosser, M and Waterhouse, F (1999) 'Relations between teachers' approaches to teaching and student's approaches to learning', *Higher Education*, **37**, pp 57–70.

Chapter 3   Teaching in Small Groups

INTRODUCTION

This chapter assumes you have been asked to teach a small group. It also assumes that the group you are to take will meet on more than one occasion and therefore will present you with the opportunity to establish and develop a productive group learning atmosphere. Small-group teaching can be a most rewarding experience. However, to achieve success you will need to plan carefully and to develop skills in group management. You should not fall into the common error of believing that discussion in groups will just happen. Even if it does, it is often directionless, unproductive, unsatisfying and perhaps threatening. To avoid these problems you will need some understanding of how groups work and how to apply a range of small group techniques to achieve your goals.

THE IMPORTANCE OF SMALL-GROUP TEACHING AND LEARNING

Teaching in small groups enjoys an important place among the teaching and learning methods commonly found in education for two rather different reasons. The first of these can be described as **social** and the other as **educational**. For many students in higher education, and especially those in the early years of their studies, the small group or tutorial provides an important social contact with peers and teachers. The value of this contact should not be underestimated as a means for students to meet and deal with people and to resolve a range of matters indirectly associated with their learning, such as difficulties with studying, course attendance and so on. Such matters will, of course, assist with the attainment of the more strictly educational objectives of your course.

Among the educational objectives that you can best achieve through students participating in small group methods are the development of higher-level intellectual skills such as reasoning and problem-solving, the development of attitudes, and the acquisition of interpersonal skills such as listening, speaking, arguing and group leadership. These skills are important to all students who will eventually become involved with other professionals, the community, learned societies and the like. As such, they are important in the process of becoming lifelong learners. The distinction between social and educational aspects of small-group teaching is rather an arbitrary one but it is important to bear it in mind when you plan for small group teaching.

WHAT IS SMALL-GROUP TEACHING?

Most of what passes for small-group teaching turns out to be little more than a lecture to a small number of students. Nor is size, within limits, a critical feature for effective small-group teaching. We believe that small-group teaching must have at least the following three characteristics:

- active participation;
- face-to-face contact;
- purposeful activity.

Active participation

The first, and perhaps the most important, characteristic of small group teaching is that teaching and learning are

brought about through discussion among **all** present. This generally implies a group size that is sufficiently small to enable each group member to contribute. Research and practical experience have established that between five and eight students is ideal for most small group teaching. You will know that many so-called small groups or tutorial groups are very much larger than this ideal. Although a group of over 20 students hardly qualifies as a small group, it is worth remembering that, with a little ingenuity, you can use many of the small group teaching procedures described in this chapter with considerable success with larger numbers of students. Generally speaking, though, in such a situation you will be looking for a technique that allows you to break the number down into subgroups for at least some of the time.

Face-to-face contact

The second characteristic of small-group teaching is that it involves face-to-face contact among all those present. You will find it difficult to conduct satisfactory small group teaching in a lecture theatre or tutorial room with students sitting in rows. Similarly, long boardroom-type tables are quite unsuitable because those present cannot see all other group members, especially those seated alongside. Effective discussion requires communication which is not only verbal but also non-verbal, involving, for example, gestures, facial expressions, eye contact and posture. This will only be achieved by sitting the group in a circle.

Purposeful activity

The third characteristic of small-group teaching is that the session must have a purpose and must develop in an orderly way. It is certainly not an occasion for idle chit-chat although, regrettably, some teaching in groups appears to be little more than this. The purposes you set for your small group can be quite wide. They include discussing a topic or a problem, and developing skills such as criticizing, analysing, problem-solving and decision-making. It is highly likely that you will wish the small-group session to achieve more than one purpose. In universities and colleges, most groups are expected to deal with a substantial amount of content. However, you will also wish to use the small-group approach to develop the higher intellectual skills of your students and even to influence their attitudes. To achieve these various purposes you will need considerable skills in managing the group and a clear plan so that the discussion will proceed in an orderly fashion towards its conclusion.

MANAGING A SMALL GROUP

Small group teaching is considerably more difficult to manage than a lecture because you must take a closer account of the students' behaviour, their difficulties and the emotional aspects of being in a group. To achieve success with a small group you must also have a clear understanding of how a group operates and how it develops. You have particular responsibilities as the initial leader of the group and your role will vary considerably, both within a session and from session to session. For instance, if you adopt an autocratic or authoritarian style of leadership (not an uncommon one) you may well have a lot of purposeful activity but there will be a limited amount of spontaneous participation. You should preferably adopt a more cooperative role where you demonstrate an expectation that the students will take responsibility for initiating discussion, providing information, asking questions, challenging statements, asking for clarification and so on. A successful group is one that can proceed purposefully without the need for constant intervention by the teacher. This is hard for most teachers to accept but is very rewarding if one recognizes that this independence is one of the key goals of small group teaching and is more important than satisfying one's own need to be deferred to as teacher and content expert.

In managing a group, there are two main factors that have to be considered. These are those relating to the **task** of the group and those relating to the **maintenance** of the group. In addition there must be a concern for the needs of each student within the group.

The tasks of the group: Tasks must be clearly defined. This is something that must be high on the agenda of the first meeting. The reason for the small group sessions and their purpose in the course must be explained. In addition, you must initiate a discussion about how you wish the group to operate, what degree of preparation you expect between group meetings, what role you intend to adopt, what roles you expect the students to assume and so on. Because such details may be quickly forgotten it is desirable to provide the student with a handout. Figure 3.1 lists some headings which may be helpful.

FIGURE 3.1 SUGGESTED HEADINGS FOR A SMALL-GROUP HANDOUT

- Course title, description and aims.
- Teacher's name and availability.
- List of students' names.
- How the group is to run (eg teacher's role, students' roles, method to be used).
- Work requirements (eg assignments, case presentations).
- Assessment arrangements.
- Reading matter.

Maintenance of the group: This refers to the achievement of a good 'climate' for discussion. It must be one that is open, trusting and supportive rather than closed, suspicious, defensive and competitive. It is important to establish that the responsibility for this factor rests with the students as well as with the teacher. The firm but pleasant handling of the loquacious or dominating students early in the session or the encouragement of the quiet student to contribute are examples of what must be achieved to produce the required environment for effective group discussion.

The successfully managed group will meet the criteria shown in Figure 3.2.

- Prevalence of a warm, accepting, non-threatening group climate.
- Learning approached as a cooperative rather than a competitive enterprise.
- Learning accepted as the major reason for the existence of the group.
- Active participation by all.
- Equal distribution of leadership functions.
- Group sessions and learning tasks are enjoyable.
- Content adequately and efficiently covered.
- Evaluation accepted as an integral part of the group's activities.
- Students attend regularly.
- Students come prepared.

STRUCTURE IN SMALL-GROUP TEACHING

We mentioned earlier the need to have a clear plan so that the group discussion will proceed with purpose and in an orderly fashion. A structured approach to the task and the allocation of the time available is a useful tool for you to consider. A simple example of such a structured discussion session is illustrated in Figure 3.3. This approach will be particularly helpful when students new to your course may not know how to interpret your simple direction to 'discuss'. The approach is suggested for any course where a reading task has been set.

Note that the structure lays out **what** is to be discussed and how much **time** is budgeted. Such a scheme is not intended to encourage undue rigidity or inflexibility, but to clarify purposes and tasks. This may seem to be a trivial matter, but it is one which creates considerable uncer-

FIGURE 3.3   STRUCTURED CASE DISCUSSION SESSION

1 PRELIMINARIES/HOUSEKEEPING MATTERS

5 MINS

2 A STUDENT PRESENTS THE INITIAL HISTORY AND EXAMINATION FINDINGS OF A WARD PATIENT   5 MINS

3 GROUP ASKED TO GENERATE HYPOTHESES AND DIAGNOSES, DISCUSS IMMEDIATE MANAGEMENT AND INITIAL INVESTIGATIONS

15 MINS

4 INFORMATION PROVIDED ON WHAT THE STUDENT (AND CONSULTANT) THOUGHT WAS THE DIAGNOSIS, WHAT WAS DONE, AND WHICH INVESTIGATIONS WERE ORDERED. GROUP DISCUSSES ANY DISPARITIES   10 MINS

5 STUDENT PRESENTS FURTHER DATA ON INVESTIGATIONS AND PROGRESS. GROUP DISCUSSES ANY DISPARITIES   10 MINS

6 GROUP LEADER OFFERS CONCLUDING REMARKS AND OPPORTUNITY FOR CLARIFICATION OF UNRESOLVED ISSUES   5 MINS

TOTAL   50 MINS

tainty for students. Keeping to a time budget is very difficult. You need to be alert to how time is being spent and whether time from one part of the plan can be transferred to an unexpected and important issue that arises during discussion.

Another structure is illustrated in Figure 3.4. This stucture includes the principle of 'snowballing' groups. From an individual task, the student progresses through a series of small groups of steadily increasing size. There are special advantages in using this structure which are worth

FIGURE 3.4   A
SNOWBALLING GROUP
DISCUSSION (AFTER
NORTHEDGE)

INDIVIDUAL WORK	10 MINS
STUDENTS READ BRIEF BACKGROUND DOCUMENT ON TOPIC, READ CASE HISTORY AND EXAMINE LABORATORY RESULTS	
WORK IN PAIRS	10 MINS
STUDENTS COMPARE UNDERSTANDINGS, CLEAR UP DIFFICULTIES, MAKE PRELIMINARY DIAGNOSIS AND DECIDE ON FURTHER TESTS	
WORK IN SMALL GROUP	15 MINS
PAIRS REPORT TO THE SMALL GROUP. GROUP DISCUSSES DIAGNOSES AND FURTHER TESTS, SEEKING AGREEMENT OR CLARIFYING DISAGREEMENTS. GROUP PREPARES REPORT FOR WHOLE GROUP	
REPORTING BACK TO WHOLE GROUP	20 MINS
EACH SMALL GROUP PRESENTS REPORT, TEACHER NOTES MAIN POINTS ON BOARD, BUTCHERS PAPER OR OVERHEAD TRANSPARENCY. AS GROUPS CONTRIBUTE, TEACHER AND STUDENTS OFFER COMMENTS. TEACHER OR STUDENTS ATTEMPT SUMMARY OF POINTS RAISED AND SOME FORM OF CONCLUSION	

noting: it does not depend on prior student preparation for success; the initial individual work brings all students to approximately the same level before discussion begins, and it ensures that everyone participates, at least in the preliminary stages.

For teachers of science students there is a wealth of stimulating examples of small group teaching methods in the book *Small Group Teaching in Undergraduate Science* by Black. In one section of this book, which discusses the teaching of intellectual skills, a broad structure is recommended, as shown in Figure 3.5.

FIGURE 3.5 *STRUCTURED SESSION FOR TEACHING INTELLECTUAL SKILLS (AFTER BLACK)*

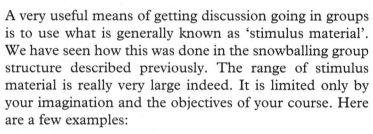

- A set of prepared problems.
- A group large enough to be divided for part of the time into four subgroups of about four students each.
- Subgroups working for about half the time on the problems.
- A brief report on the work of each group.
- Class discussion based on the group's reports.

INTRODUCING STIMULUS MATERIALS

A very useful means of getting discussion going in groups is to use what is generally known as 'stimulus material'. We have seen how this was done in the snowballing group structure described previously. The range of stimulus material is really very large indeed. It is limited only by your imagination and the objectives of your course. Here are a few examples:

- A short multiple-choice test (ambiguous items work well in small groups.
- A case study.
- A short open-ended situation on video, such as a person-to-person encounter.
- A patient in a medical or dental course.
- Observation of a role-play.
- Visual materials (eg photographs, slides, specimens, real objectives, charts, diagrams, statistical data).
- An audio-recording (eg an interview, sounds, a segment of a radio broadcast).
- A student's written report on a project, field-work or laboratory-work.
- Material displayed by computer, possibly on the World Wide Web.
- A journal article or other written material, such as an abstract. (The paper by Moore gives an interesting example of this approach using extracts from literary works to help students understand the broader

cultural, philosophical, ethical and personal issues of the subject under study. The added benefit, of course, is a broadening of the educational experience of students.)

ALTERNATIVE SMALL-GROUP DISCUSSION TECHNIQUES

As with any other aspects of teaching, it is helpful to have a variety of techniques at one's fingertips in order to introduce variety or to suit a particular situation. Such techniques include:

- one-to-one discussion;
- buzz groups;
- brainstorming;
- role-playing;
- plenary session.

One-to-one discussion

This is a very effective technique which can be used with a group of almost any size. It is particularly useful as an 'ice-breaker' when the group first meets, and is valuable for enhancing listening skills. It can also be used to discuss controversial or ethical issues so that forceful individuals with strong opinions will be prevented from dominating the discussion: they will also be required to listen to other opinions and express them to the whole group. (See Figure 3.6.)

FIGURE 3.6   CONDUCTING
A ONE-TO-ONE DISCUSSION

A
Procedure
- Group members (preferably including the teacher) divide into pairs and each person is designated 'A' or 'B'.
- Person A talks to person B for an **uninterrupted** period of 3–5 minutes on the topic for discussion.

- Person B listens and avoids prompting or questioning.
- Roles are reversed with B talking to A.
- At the conclusion the group reassembles.
- Each person, in turn, introduces themselves before introducing the person to whom they were speaking. They then briefly paraphrase what was said by that person.

B **Use as ice-breaker**
- Group members are asked to respond to a question such as 'Tell me something about yourself' or 'What do you expect to learn from this course?'.

C **General use**
- Group members respond to appropriate questioning, eg 'What is your opinion about...?'.

It is useful to insist on the no interruption rule (though not so much when used as an ice-breaker). Prolonged periods of silence may ensue but person A will be using this time for uninterrupted thinking, a luxury not available in most situations. Often the first superficial response to a question will be changed after deeper consideration.

Buzz groups

These are particularly helpful to encourage maximum participation at one time. It is therefore especially useful when groups are large, or if too many people are trying to contribute at once or, alternatively, if shyness is inhibiting several students. (See Figure 3.7.)

FIGURE 3.7   CONDUCTING
A BUZZ GROUP

Procedure
- The group is divided into subgroups of 3–4 students.
- Discussion occurs for a few minutes (the term 'buzz' comes from the hive of verbal activity!).
- A clear task must be set.
- Each subgroup reports back to the whole group.

Brainstorming

This is a technique that you should consider when you wish to encourage wide and creative thinking about a problem. It is also valuable when highly critical group members (including perhaps yourself?) appear to be inhibiting discussion. If used frequently, it trains students to think up ideas before they are dismissed or criticized. The key to successful brainstorming is to separate the generation of ideas, or possible solutions to a problem, from the evaluation of these ideas or solutions. (See Figure 3.8.) Before using brainstorming, we suggest you have a look at Stein's book on creativity.

FIGURE 3.8   CONDUCTING A
BRAINSTORMING SESSION

Procedure
- Explain these rules of brainstorming to the group:
  - criticism is ruled out during the idea generation stage;
  - all ideas are welcome;
  - quantity of ideas is the aim (so as to improve the chances of good ideas coming up);
  - combination and improvement of ideas will be sought once all new ideas are obtained.
- State the problem to the group.
- A period of silent thought is allowed during which students write down their ideas.
- Ideas are then recorded (in a round-robin format) on a blackboard, overhead transparency or flipchart for all to see.
- When **all** ideas are listed, and combination and improvement of ideas are complete, discussion and evaluation commences.

Role-playing

This is a powerful and underused technique. It is very valuable in teaching interpersonal communication skills, particularly in areas with a high emotional content. It has been found to be helpful in changing perceptions and in developing empathy. It is not a technique to use without some experience so you should arrange to sit in on a role-play session before using it in your own course. In this regard, colleagues teaching psychology, education, psychiatry or counselling should be able to help you, as will the Green Guide by Ernington.

FIGURE 3.9 CONDUCTING A ROLE-PLAY

Procedure
- Explain the nature and purpose of the exercise.
- Define the setting and situation.
- Select students to act out roles.
- Provide players with a realistic description of the role or even a script. Allow time for them to prepare and, if necessary, practise.
- Specify observational tasks for non-players.
- Allow sufficient time for the role-play.
- Discuss and explore the experience with players and observers.

Plenary session

In many group teaching situations, and indeed at conferences and workshops, subgroups must report back to the larger group. This reporting back can be tedious and often involves only the subgroup leaders who may present a very distorted view of what happened. The plenary session method may help you with these problems. (See Figure 3.10.)

FIGURE 3.10 CONDUCTING A PLENARY SESSION

Procedure
- Subgroups sit together facing other subgroups.
- The chair of subgroup B invites the chair of subgroup A to briefly report the substance of the discussion in subgroup A.

- The chair of subgroup B then invites members of subgroups B, C, D etc to ask questions of any member of group A.
- After 10 minutes the chair of subgroup C invites the chair of B to report on the discussion in subgroup B and the process is repeated for each subgroup.
- The 10-minute (or other) time limit must be adhered to strictly.

USING TECHNOLOGY FOR TEACHING SMALL GROUPS

By combining computers and communication technology, you can make fundamental changes to the way you present and distribute material and interact with your students. By using these technologies, the distinctions between large- and small-group teaching tend to break down, so it is more useful to discuss the matter separately, which we do in Chapter 4.

However, some examples of the ways in which technology can be used to support small-group teaching are:

- by using electronic mail (e-mail) to communicate with one or more students;
- through electronic discussion groups;
- by adopting conferencing techniques using computer, sound and video.

Implementing electronic teaching is very different to other approaches in many ways. For instance, uninitiated colleagues will be totally uncomprehending if you object to being interrupted when you are working at your computer by saying that you are 'teaching'!

One fundamental different between face-to-face teaching and interacting online is that you will be interacting with what is known as a 'virtual' group. This means that the group does not exist as an entity at any one time or place, but that it is dispersed both in time (within limits) and place, and that the group interacts 'asynchronously' (at different times). Furthermore, there are different rules of behaviour for electronic communication known colloquially as 'netiquette' which both you and your students should observe. To learn more about this topic you can search for it on the World Wide Web. A very good overview is provided at: http:www.albion.com/ netiquette/book/index.html or in the book *Netiquette* by Virginia Shea, published by Albion Books in 1994.

WHEN THINGS GO WRONG

You will undoubtedly have a variety of difficulties to deal with in your group sessions. For example, you might decide to ignore the behaviour of a sleeping student or an amorous couple in the back row of a lecture class, providing it was not disruptive, but it would be impossible to do so in a small group. How you resolve problems with the working of the group is critical. An authoritarian approach would almost certainly destroy any chance of establishing the cooperative climate we believe to be essential. It is generally more appropriate to raise the problem with the group and ask them for their help with a solution.

One of your main roles as a group leader is to be sensitive to the group and the individuals within it. Research has identified a number of difficulties that students commonly experience. These are connected with:

● making a contribution to the discussion;
● understanding the conventions of group work and acceptable modes of behaviour;
● knowing enough to contribute to the discussion;
● being assessed.

These difficulties frequently get in the way of productive discussion. They tend to be due to genuine confusion on the part of students, combined with a fear of exposing their ignorance in front of the teacher and their peers. It is therefore essential for you to clarify the purpose of the group and the way in which students are to enter into the discussion. Their previous experience of small group sessions might lead them to see the occasion as only a threatening question-and-answer session. They must learn that ignorance is a relative term and that their degree of ignorance must be recognized and explored before effective learning can begin. A willingness by the teacher to admit ignorance and demonstrate an appropriate way of dealing with it will be very reassuring to many students.

Confusion in the students' minds about how they are being assessed can also cause difficulties. Generally speaking, assessing contributions to discussion is inhibiting and should be avoided. If you do not have discretion in this matter then at least make it quite clear what criteria you are looking for in your assessment. Should you be able to determine your own assessment policy then the following criteria are worth considering:

- require attendance at all (or a specified proportion of) group meetings as a prerequisite;
- set formal written work, eg a major essay, a series of short papers, a case analysis;
- set a group-based task, eg keeping an account of the work done by the group.

The teacher's perceptions of group difficulties may not necessarily match those of the students. A discussion with the group about how they think things are going or the administration of a short questionnaire are ways of seeking feedback.

Once the group is operating it is important to monitor it. You must be sensitive to the emotional responses of the group and to the behaviour of individual students. When things go wrong, you will find it helpful to access the wisdom of experienced practitioners. The book by Richard Tiberius is a recommended resource.

EVALUATING SMALL-GROUP TEACHING

Evaluation implies collecting information about your teaching and then making judgements based on that information. Making judgements based on what one student says, or on rumour or intuition, is simply not good enough. You must collect information in a way that is likely to lead to valid judgements. However, constant evaluation of small-group activities is not recommended as it may inhibit the development and working of the group. Evaluation may be of two types: informal or formal.

FIGURE 3.11 EXAMPLE OF TUTORIAL QUESTIONNAIRE (ADVISORY CENTRE FOR UNIVERSITY EDUCATION, UNIVERSITY OF ADELAIDE)

Name .... Course ....

Please indicate your thoughts about the tutorial given by this particular tutor.

Indicate your present thoughts by means of a tick on the four-point scale.

(A) **The tutor**

good group leader	- - - -	poor group leader
fits into the group	- - - -	too forceful
likes opinions questioned	- - - -	discourages the questioning of opinions
patient	- - - -	impatient
never sarcastic	- - - -	sarcastic
lively	- - - -	monotonous
pleasant manner	- - - -	unpleasant manner
interested in students	- - - -	not interested in students
interested in my ideas	- - - -	not interested in my ideas
interested in me as an individual	- - - -	does not know me
encourages me to discuss problems	- - - -	unable to discuss problems
treats me as an equal	- - - -	treats me as a subordinate
clearly audible	- - - -	mumbles
stresses important material	- - - -	all material seems the same

makes good use of examples
and illustrations - - - - never gives examples
explanations clear and
understandable - - - - quite incomprehensible
appears confident - - - - not confident

(B) **The tutorials**

well organized	- - - -	muddled
good progression	- - - -	poor progression
well prepared	- - - -	not well prepared
time well spent	- - - -	a waste of time
new material covered	- - - -	merely repeat lecture material
have thrown new light on lecture course	- - - -	irrelevant to understanding of lecture course
overcome difficulties encountered in lectures	- - - -	difficulties not dealt with

(C) **The student's response**

I am fully aware of my progress	- - - -	I seem to be 'working in the dark'
I enjoy contributing	- - - -	I try to say nothing
I look forward to the tutorials	- - - -	I would prefer not to attend
I have learnt a lot	- - - -	I have learnt nothing
I am more inclined to continue with the subject	- - - -	I have developed an aversion to the subject

Advice or suggestions for the future should be written on the back.

Informal evaluation: This can proceed from your careful reflection of what happened during your time with the group. You may do this by considering a number of criteria which you feel are important. For example, you may be interested in the distribution of discussion among group members, the quality of contribution, the amount of your own talk, whether the purpose of the session was achieved and so on. Of course, your reflections will be biased and it is wise to seek confirmation by questioning students from time to time. However, the importance of informal evaluations lies in your commitment to turn these reflections into improvements. If you are concerned with your own performance, discussion with the group may be very helpful.

Formal evaluation: One formal approach to evaluation has already been described, the evaluation discussion.

Other approaches include the use of questionnaires and the analysis of video-recordings of the group at work. Standard questionnaires are available which seek student responses to a set number of questions. An example is shown in Figure 3.11.

Although such standard questionnaires can be useful, you may find it more beneficial to design one that contributes more directly to answering questions which relate to your own course and concerns. As questionnaire design is a tricky business, it is recommended that you seek the assistance of a teaching unit. The analysis of videotapes of your group at work is also a task which would require the expertise of someone from a teaching unit or a relevant teaching department such as psychology.

Evaluation discussion

Perhaps a better approach is to use the potential of small-group interaction as a tool of evaluation. We find the evaluation discussion technique to be very useful (see Figure 3.12). An advantage of evaluation discussion is that it can give you feedback on what students are learning, how they feel about their learning and your teaching.

FIGURE 3.12   CONDUCTING AN EVALUATION DISCUSSION

Procedure
- Before the group meeting students are asked to write a 1–2 page evaluation of the group's work focusing equally on their intellectual and emotional reactions to the **processes** of teaching and **what** they are learning.
- Each student reads this evaluation to the group.
- Each member of the group is then free to ask questions, agree or disagree, or to comment.

For success you must be sure to create a non-judgemental atmosphere of acceptance where negative as well as positive information can be freely given. Listen rather than react!

GUIDED READING

For a wide-ranging discussion of the purposes and techniques of small group teaching we suggest you turn to the collection of papers edited by D Blight: *Teach Thinking by Discussion*, SRHE/NFER-Nelson, Guildford, UK, 1986. This monograph also provides a good introduction to the research literature on small groups. Also, *Small Group Teaching: A troubleshooting guide* by Richard Tiberius (Kogan Page, London, 1999) is recommended.

Another excellent guide, to both the theory and the practice of group work, is D Jacques, *Learning in Groups* (Second Edition, Kogan Page, London, 1991).

Books and journals referred to in this chapter:

Black, P J *et al*, (1977) *Small Group Teaching in Undergraduate Science*, Nuffield Foundation/Heinemann, UK.

Ernington, E (1997) *Role Play*, HERDSA Green Guide No. 21. (This is available from HERDSA, PO Box 516, Jamieson ACT 2614, Australia.)

Moore, A R (1976) 'Medical humanities – a new medical adventure', *New England Journal of Medicine*, **295**, pp 1479–80.

Northedge, A (1975) 'Learning through discussion at the Open University', *Teaching at a Distance*, **2**, pp 10–17.

Chapter 4   Teaching in Large Groups

INTRODUCTION

Large-group teaching is often thought of as the same as lecturing. While these two methods share some similarities, we want to encourage you to move away from the idea of 'lecturing' to a group of passive students towards the idea of student-centred, active learning. Large-group teaching, carefully organized and implemented, uses a combination of strategies that cause your students to engage enthusiastically in active learning, can provide you with immediate feedback on their learning and builds a productive and scholarly relationship with students – even in very large classes numbering hundreds of students.

In fact, the whole idea of teaching large groups is changing at a rapid pace because the growth in use of computer and communications technology has made the teaching of very large 'virtual' classes a reality. In this scenario, the teacher's role changes from that of a presenter to that of a constructor of learning resources, and a guide and manager of learning.

Why do we want to support you in this move towards student-centred learning? Because the evidence continues to mount that, although the lecture is as effective as other methods in transmitting information (but not *more* effective), it is not as effective as other methods in stimulating thinking, inspiring interest in a subject, teaching behavioural skills, or changing attitudes. These are among the objectives that many university teachers aspire to when they lecture. On the other hand, if we seriously wish to foster lifelong-learning skills and attitudes among our students, one of the worst things we can do is to encourage and reward the kinds of passivity that the lecture method commonly provides.

THE CONTEXT OF LARGE-GROUP TEACHING

An important preliminary step in your preparation is to find out as much as you can about the context of your teaching in the overall teaching programme or course. Unfortunately, this context is often ill-defined and may be only a title in a long list of topics given out by the department or school.

However, do try to find out as much as you can about the context. This means enquiring about such things as:

- what students have been taught (and what they may know);
- what the purpose of your teaching session is to be;
- what resources, such as library materials, are available for students;
- what the assessment arrangements for the course or unit are;
- what methods have been used to teach students in the past.

This last point is the most important. You may wish, after reading this chapter, to try out some new ideas with students. Beware! Students do appreciate good teaching but may resent the use of some techniques that seem irrelevant to their purposes, to the course aims, and to the way their learning is assessed. When introducing new learning and teaching techniques, you must carefully explain the purpose of them to students. Be prepared for some resistance, especially from senior students, if they do not appreciate the connection between the techniques and the assessment arrangements.

The course controller, curriculum committee, head of department and other teachers in the course are all potential sources of advice and assistance to you. However, do not be surprised if you are told that you are the expert and that it is your responsibility to know what students ought to be taught! If this happens, you should insist on some help to review what has happened in the past. To do otherwise is to teach in an academic vacuum.

WHAT ABOUT NON-TRADITIONAL STUDENTS?

A declining proportion of university students may be entering directly from local secondary schools. Given the growing numbers of non-traditional students – international students, students with disabilities, transfer students, students from different cultural and linguistic backgrounds, and mature-age students – it is important that you note the composition of your class and consider this in your planning. What can be done? An essential starting point is to address the educational principles outlined in our Statement. Teaching based on these principles is likely to be good teaching for *all* students in your class, so everyone benefits.

In addition, you can assist your students from diverse backgrounds by instituting practices that provide modelling, resources for increased comprehension and enhanced opportunities for social contact.

Modelling the kinds of learning objectives you have will be important for all students, including those who come from cultures where the traditional authority of teachers and authors is strongly valued and not to be questioned. So, plan to model critical or analytical thinking, for example, by publicly questioning a set text and explicitly demonstrating through your own thinking approaches the ways in which scholars in your discipline test the validity of claims made.

Resources for increased comprehension will be welcomed by the majority of your class, but particularly those students for whom the language of instruction is not their first language, and for hearing and sight-impaired students. What can you do? A short list would include:

- present an overview and structure to each session;
- include concrete examples of the principles you are teaching;
- link one session to the next and to the one preceding it;
- use clear, large, legible overheads or slides;
- use handouts;
- provide an outline of the teaching session;
- audiotape classes and maintain a tape library;
- post class notes on the Internet or on an intranet; and
- indicate supporting references in books and journals, stating why each reference is important or how it relates to the topic.

Using technology when teaching large groups can also be a valid strategy to address some of these issues. See below for ideas on how you might proceed with this.

Social contact will be achieved in large-group teaching when you use some of the group-based approaches described here. One of the most under-used resources in higher education is the students themselves, so plan ways in which you might constructively use the experience and knowledge of particular students or groups of students in your teaching. Now only will the learning be enriched, but an opportunity for some social contact between students will arise.

PREPARING FOR LARGE-GROUP TEACHING

What is the purpose of your teaching?

Having clarified the context of your large-group teaching session you need to ask yourself 'What is its purpose?'.

This is a question you should always ask so that you have a clear idea about matching ends with means.

A possible range of answers is given below, many of which will overlap:

- To **encourage** thinking skills. *Examples:* Interpretation of a set of statistical data; evaluation of an engineering proposal; criticism of a literary work, a journal article or medical treatment plan; application of earlier learning to a novel situation.
- To **construct** an academic argument. *Example:* Presentation of the pros and cons of an argument with respect to a public-policy issue.
- To **present** students with information about a subject. *Example:* A review and commentary on the research on a particular subject.
- To **demonstrate** a procedure, a way of thinking, or approach to problem solving. *Examples:* Lead students through a line of reasoning about a problem; demonstrate (with suitable apparatus) a physical process or phenomenon.

Resolving the purpose of your large-group teaching will be a useful benchmark throughout the process of preparation, presentation and final evaluation.

After clarifying the context and purpose to the best of your ability, the time has come to get down to some detailed planning. The best way to start is to write down the purpose(s) of your teaching. We say 'write down' advisedly because nothing clarifies the mind more than putting pen to paper!

Identify the content

Set about identifying the content. We suggest you start by jotting down the main ideas, theories and examples that come to mind regarding the central purpose of your teaching session. This should be spontaneously, without any particular concern for the order in which you may eventually wish to organize your material. Figure 4.1 illustrates a way of doing this that has been found to be helpful by individuals attending our courses for new academic staff.

FIGURE 4.1 METHOD OF IDENTIFYING THE CONTENT FOR A LECTURE (AFTER BUZAN, 1988)

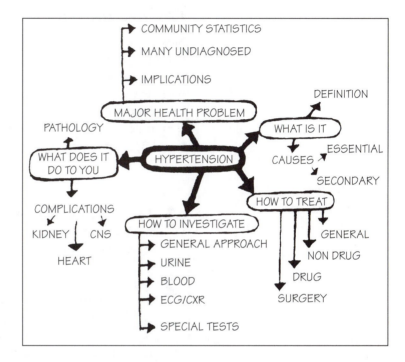

The topic (in the example, taken from a medical lecture on hypertension) is placed in the centre of the paper and the main points to be made are written down as indicated. After the main ideas have been identified, further points will tend to branch out as you think more carefully about them. This process should be continued until you have exhausted all your ideas. You may at this stage find that you need to read about some of the ideas in order to refine them or to bring yourself up to date.

During this exercise you will find that illustrative examples of key points come to mind. Jot these down too. In addition, you should be on the look out for illustrations from which you might prepare audiovisual aids and teaching materials. Appropriate jokes or cartoons may be collected during this exercise. And, most importantly, make a note of short activities or exercises that you can use as a basis for student activity.

Finalize the plan

Now you must finalize your teaching plan. The rough content plan must be transformed into a structure that follows some kind of logical sequence. There is no single best way of doing so, but you may prefer a formal structure from which to work. The important point is to have a structure – make this clear to students when you are teaching. One such structure is shown in Figure 4.2.

FIGURE 4.2   LARGE-GROUP TEACHING PLAN

1 Introduction and overview
   a. Describe the purpose of the session.
   b. Outline the key areas to be covered.

2 First key point
   a. Development of ideas.
   b. Use of examples.
   c. Restatement of first key point.
   d. Task/exercise/question for students.

3 Second key point
   a. Development of ideas.
   b. Use of examples.
   c. Restatement of first and second points.
   d. Task/exercise/question for students.

4 Third key point
   a. Development of ideas.
   b. Use of examples.
   c. Restatement of first, second and third points.
   d. Task/exercise/question for students.

5 Summary and conclusion

This is the classical content-orientated plan. We hope that you may wish to be more ambitious and use other plans which have the potential to demonstrate more effectively how knowledge is discovered and organized in your discipline. These plans require extra thought but, done well, are likely to be rewarding to both you and your students.

Let us consider two examples. The first example is called the **comparative plan**. If you wished to develop an understanding of the comparisons between A and B, you could start with:

- Introduction.
- First major point: details about A.
- Second major point: details about B.
- Third major point: criteria for comparison.
- Fourth major point: comparisons and contrasts.
- Summary and conclusions.

A second adaptation of the basic structure is the **problem-focused plan**. It can be structured as follows:

- Introduction: statement of the problem and overview of range of solutions.
- First major point: solution I.
- Second major point: solution II.
- Third major point: solution III.
- Fourth major point: comparison of ease, validity or appropriateness.
- Summary and conclusions.

The third adaptation is the **academic-argument plan**. The order in which you place arguments in this structure appears to be critical. The order suggested is:

- Introduction: overview of teacher's position and supporting arguments.
- First major point: presentation of counter-arguments.
- Second major point: discussion/refutation of counter-arguments.

- Third major point: arguments in favour of teacher's position.
- Conclusion: restatement of teacher's position.

These examples imply that all large-group sessions are complete in themselves. In reality, of course, this may not be the case. Most will be part of a series on a particular topic or theme. Consequently, they will need to be linked together to provide continuity from one session to the next. In other words, you will need to modify the plans suggested above to suit the demands of your teaching as it proceeds through the series.

The plans illustrate the general question that you will have to answer as you organize your material. That question is 'How will I sequence the ideas I wish to present?'. Sometimes the sequence might be indicated by the nature of the material to be presented. However, apparently logical sequences may not always be optimal for student learning and you should give some thought to the ways in which student interest, their knowledge and their approaches to learning suggest sequences of presentation. Some possible sequences are:

- Proceed from observations of reality (such as a brief in-class activity eg, a case study, an exercise or short test, a short film or video, a Classroom Assessment Technique (see below) or a demonstration) to abstract ideas, theories and principles. This is sometimes called an 'inductive' approach to teaching.
- Proceed from generalizations to particular examples and applications. This is a 'deductive' approach – a reversal of the inductive sequence outlined above.
- Proceed from simple ideas and applications to more complex ones.
- Proceed from what students can be expected to know to what students do not know.
- Proceed from common misconceptions to explanation and clarification.
- Proceed from a whole view to a more detailed view.

PRESENTING THE LARGE-GROUP TEACHING SESSION

Having decided what you intend to teach, you must now give careful attention to how you are going to present it to the students. Let us assume that it is to be your first contact with this group of students. You may wish to obtain their attention initially by devising an arresting opening. Ways of doing this are limited only by your personality and imagination. An appropriate joke, a movie clip, an anecdote, a quotation or a discussion with a few of the group may generate interest.

However, it must be borne in mind that the attention of the students ought to be engaged by the material rather than the personality of the teacher. The danger of the latter has become known as the 'Dr Fox effect', an expression derived from an experiment in which an actor (Dr Fox) gave a lecture comprising meaningless double-talk which fooled experienced listeners into believing that they had participated in a worthwhile and stimulating learning experience.

Starting the session

Particular attention needs to be given to the way you begin. For many teachers, this is the most difficult aspect of teaching a large group. It is essential to decide before-hand exactly how you intend to start. Do not leave this decision until you are facing the students. Perhaps the easiest way to start is to explain the purpose of the teaching session and how it is organized. An outline on the board or on a transparency showing your teaching plan is a good way of doing this. Such visual material will take attention away from yourself, give you something to talk to and allow you to settle down. Writing the plan on the board gives students a permanent reminder of the structure of your session.

Once you become more confident, other issues should be considered. It is good practice to arrive early and chat with some of the students to establish their level of previous knowledge. Alternatively, you can start by asking a few pertinent questions, taking care that this is done in a non-threatening manner. Should you establish that serious deficiencies in knowledge are present, you must be flexible enough to try and correct them rather than continue regardless.

Varying the format

You should now give attention to the body of the large-group session. Student attention must be considered. A purely verbal presentation will be ineffective and will contribute to a fall-off in the level of attention. You should therefore be planning ways of incorporating some of the techniques described in the next section. Figure 4.3 shows us that levels of attention and learning will fall progressively. No more than 20 minutes should go by before the students are given a learning activity or before the teaching technique is significantly altered. Ways of doing this include posing questions or testing the students, generating discussion among students or using an audiovisual aid. These active-learning strategies are discussed in more detail later.

FIGURE 4.3   HYPOTHESIZED PATTERN OF STUDENT LEVEL OF PERFORMANCE SHOWING A PROGRESSIVE FALL IN ATTENTION AND LEARNING DURING AN UNINTERRUPTED LECTURE AND CONTRASTING THIS WITH THE GAIN OBTAINED FROM INTRODUCING A REST PERIOD (AFTER BLIGH, 1998)

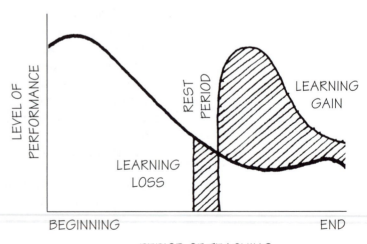

Finishing the session

The conclusion is as important as the introduction. Your closing comments should also be well prepared. The last things you say are the ones that students are most likely to remember. The conclusion presents an opportunity to reiterate the key points you hope to have made. You may also wish to direct students to additional reading at this point, but be reasonable in your expectations and give them a clear indication of what is essential and *why* it is essential, as opposed to what you think is merely desirable. Providing students with a couple of minutes before the conclusion to consolidate and read their notes is a worthwhile technique to use from time to time.

Rehearsal and check

Some of the best teachers we know find it very helpful to rehearse or to try out some parts of their teaching, so this may be even more important for the less experienced. However, the purpose of a rehearsal should not be to become word perfect, and it is impossible to rehearse the outcomes of activities that you give to your students. A rehearsal will often reveal that you are attempting to cram too much into the given time and that some of your visual aids are poorly prepared or difficult to see from the back of the lecture space. The value of a rehearsal will be much enhanced if you invite a colleague to act as the audience and provide critical comments as well as helping you to check out projectors, seating, lighting, air conditioning and other physical considerations.

In many institutions, you will have access to courses on teaching methods. Overcome your natural reticence and enrol. It is likely that one component of the course will give you the opportunity of viewing your teaching technique on video. The unit running the course may also provide an individual to come and observe your teaching, giving you the expert feedback that you may not always get from a colleague.

Some personal considerations about anxiety when teaching large groups

When you are satisfied that you have attended adequately to the kinds of things discussed above, you will find it helpful to reflect on some matters of personal preparation for your teaching. Paramount among these considerations is dealing with nervousness – both before and during your large-group session.

Most teachers, speakers and actors confess to feeling anxious before 'going onstage' and, curiously, this does not always manifest itself in the ways that the less experienced imagine. If you are thoroughly prepared, much of the potential for nervousness will have been eliminated. Also, you should keep in mind that a certain level of anxiety is desirable to ensure that you perform well!

One writer on higher education, Christine Overall, has described the commonly experienced anxiety in terms of 'feeling fraudulent'. She suggests that a way of managing this feeling is to act *as if* you know what you are doing, and to display the confidence and authority to do what you need to do. In the large group session, this may mean looking at the audience, smiling, handling audiovisual equipment confidently, being very clear and firm about instructions for active-learning tasks, knowing what you will say and do at the beginning and end of your session and so on.

Apart from being thoroughly prepared, there are a number of 'dos and don'ts' to keep in mind.

- Don't allow yourself to conjure up visions of mistakes and disasters. Think positively. Imagine an interested and appreciative audience, the achievement of the goals you set for yourself and your students and being in control of the situation.
- Practise some relaxation exercises and deep breathing. Consult one of the numerous booklets or cassettes on this topic or attend a relaxation class if you think it might help.

● If you can, plan on arriving at the lecture room early enough to ensure everything is in order and to allow time to talk to one or two of the students in the class about their work. This approach not only serves as a valuable 'bridge' between you and your students, but also can be very helpful in meeting some of their needs and understanding their difficulties, which you might be able to incorporate into your teaching.

WHAT ACTIVE-LEARNING STRATEGIES ARE AVAILABLE?

Active learning stands in contrast to much of what passes for 'learning' in large lecture classes – it is lively, dynamic, engaging and full of life. It is a basis from which lifelong-learning skills can be developed. Active learning is often defined in contrast to the worst of traditional teaching where the teacher is active and the student is the passive recipient. Specifically, active learning occurs when you use strategies to ensure that elements of student activity – which basically involves talking, reading, writing, thinking, or doing something – for example, solving a problem. These activities might be done alone, in pairs of students, or in small groups of up to about four.

There are several levels at which we would encourage you to plan for student activity. At the most basic level, we have already stressed how variety in the presentation is essential in maintaining attention and therefore the possibility of students engaging with the material.

Variations in your manner and style

It is important that you feel comfortable with the way you present your session. However, you should not limit your manner and style. Changes in the volume and rate of speech, the use of silence, maintenance of eye contact with the class and movement away from the lectern to create a less formal relationship should all be considered.

Active participation

A powerful way of enhancing learning is to devise situations that require the students to interact with you or with each other. Questions are the simplest form of interaction. Many teachers ask for questions at the end of their presentation, but most are disappointed in the student response. Others direct questions at students but, unless the teacher is very careful, the dominant emotion will be one of fear. It is therefore preferable to create a situation in which all students answer the questions and individuals are not placed in the foreground.

You may wish to prepare a question in the form of a multiple-choice or true/false item that can be projected as a slide or an overhead transparency. Asking for a show of hands for each alternative answer to the question can check understanding. You should follow up by explaining why each alternative is or is not a suitable answer. The time required for this will usually be about five to seven minutes (one to two minutes to answer the question, four to five minutes to give feedback on the correct and incorrect answers).

An alternative is having students ask questions. Again, if you ask 'Are there any questions?', silence is the likely response because individuals do not generally like to be in the foreground, particularly in very large classes. But if you ask students to write a question on paper and turn it in, you can then address some or all of these in a relatively anonymous and non-threatening way.

Small-group activity within a large group is not commonly attempted, even though it is simple to arrange for a large number of students in a theatre of any size. Once you try it out, you may find it so exciting to hear the steady hum of students actually discussing your subject that you will never again feel comfortable giving a didactic lecture! The general approach is to break down the class into small groups, using a judicious rearrangement of seating if necessary. Small groups of two to four people

may be formed among neighbours without any move-ment, while larger groups may be formed quickly by two to four students in one row turning to form a group with students in the row behind. If a substantial amount of discussion time is planned, it might be best to form the groups at the beginning of the session and ask them to spread themselves out to use up the whole lecture theatre space. The selection of the most appropriate type of groups will largely depend on what you wish to achieve. Small groups may be asked to discuss a limited topic for a few minutes (sometimes called 'buzz' groups) or to consider broader topics for a longer period of time. You may then wish to allow all or some of the groups to report back to you. This is a very useful exercise when problems are given to the students to solve and when a variety of different responses can be expected. Some more specific examples of small-group activity are now discussed.

One-to-one discussion is a particularly valuable tech-nique in a situation where you might wish all the class to consider a very emotive or challenging concept. This method is described in detail in Chapter 3 on small-group teaching.

Reading or problem-solving activities may be intro-duced. These can involve a combination of individual study and small-group discussion. There are many varia-tions on this strategy.

One example of this is the situation in which students are instructed to bring their text, or a handout is provided, consisting of an article, a summary, a quotation, a set of diagrams or a set of equations. A directed-reading or problem-solving task is set. This task should involve the students for five to ten minutes. At the end of this period of individual work, students are instructed to discuss something with the person beside them. They may be asked to compare answers, draw conclusions, raise issues, identify misunderstandings or make evaluative judge-ments. The students are then asked for feedback.

Depending on the size of the group, you could ask for reports from all or some of the pairs, have pairs report to another pair and seek general reports from these larger groups, or have a show of hands to questions or issues that you have identified as you moved around the class during the discussion phase. Alternatively, you could ask students to write responses, then collect these and collate the information after the session as a basis for your teaching in the next session. Conclude by drawing ideas together, summing up, or whatever is appropriate to the task you set them.

Whatever you do – and this is critical – thoroughly plan the activity. Clearly structure the time and the tasks set, and stick to your plan (unless there are very good reasons to change). Your instructions, including the time available and tasks to be carried out, should be clearly displayed on a handout or on the board for ready reference during the exercise.

Brainstorming is a technique that can be modified for use in large-group teaching. It can be of value at the beginning to stimulate interest in the topic to be discussed. The students are presented with an issue or a problem and are asked to contribute as many ideas or solutions as they can. All contributions are accepted without comment or judgement on their merits and are written on the board or on an overhead transparency. This approach encourages 'lateral' or 'divergent' thinking. One of us has successfully used this technique with a class of 120 at the beginning of a lecture. The session commenced with a request for the class to put forward their suggestions in response to a question. These suggestions were then categorized and used as a basis for further discussion in an environment where the students were the initiators of discussion points. Brainstorming is discussed further in the chapter on small-group teaching.

Classroom Assessment Techniques (CATs) are a relatively recent innovation that we would encourage you to use with your students. These techniques stimulate active learning, but most importantly help teachers to gather useful information on what, how much and how well their students are learning. The simplest and most popular CAT is the 'minute paper'. In this technique, the teacher stops two or three minutes early and asks students to write anonymous brief responses to a question such as: 'What was the most important thing you learnt in this class?' or 'What important question remains unanswered?' Papers are collected and reviewed by the teacher prior to the next class meeting at which time feedback may be given or points clarified.

Another CAT is the 'pro and con grid'. This technique assists in the development of thinking skills by encouraging students to go beyond initial reactions to an issue. In response to a suitable prompt or question, students write out a specified number of pros and cons or advantages and disadvantages. These can then be discussed in small groups, analysed in class, or analysed by you prior to the next class session. We strongly recommend the book by Angelo and Cross on classroom assessment – details are provided at the end of this chapter.

Student note taking

The research in this area generally supports the view that note taking should be encouraged. It is a process that requires student attention and activity. The teacher can assist this process by providing a structure for material that is complex. Diagrams and other schematic representations may be more valuable than simple prose.

USING TEACHING MATERIALS AND TECHNOLOGY

Educational issues and the technical aspects of preparing and using teaching aids and materials is discussed in detail in Chapter 7. This section will discuss their use in large group teaching for a variety of purposes including illustrating the structure, providing information and examples, stimulating interest and activity and providing variety. The aids most likely to be used are handouts, the board, overhead transparencies, slides and videos.

Handouts must serve a useful purpose and be used during the teaching session so that students are familiar with their content and do not simply file them away. Handouts may be valuable as a guide to the structure of your session and, in such cases, may be very similar in content to the teaching plan. A handout that acts as a guide to the structure of the session should be given out at the beginning. Alternatively, you may wish to use a handout to provide detailed information on an area that has not been covered well in standard student texts or an area not covered in detail in your teaching. Such handouts might be given out at the end of the session. Handouts may also be used to guide further study and to provide references for additional reading. Whenever you distribute handouts, it is essential that you use them in some way *with* your students.

Blackboards (which are usually green these days) and **whiteboards** are still very widely used and we urge you to look at the information in Chapter 7 about their preparation and use. Clear, legible and well-planned use of these basic aids is a delight to see and they remain valuable allies in assisting you to communicate with your students. They are especially valuable for displaying an outline of your session, for recording feedback from students in response to questions you may have raised and for setting out essential and new spellings or formulae.

The **overhead projector** is widely used in teaching. An overhead transparency is particularly useful for giving outlines and listing key points. A blank sheet of paper can be used to reveal the points in sequence. A pen or pencil placed on the transparency itself should be used to direct the students' attention to the appropriate point rather than using the pointer on the screen. Information may be added to the transparency with a felt pen as the teaching proceeds. We have found that the value of the overhead is seriously reduced by four common practices. Firstly, when too much information is included on each transparency. Secondly, when the teacher works through the material too quickly or talks about something different while students are trying to read and take notes from the screen. Thirdly, when the transparency is carelessly positioned or is out of focus. Fourthly, and the most common abuse, is when the material on transparencies is far too small to be read by students.

The **35 mm slide** is still used and some teachers build up an extensive collection. However, many teachers are incorporating their slides into Microsoft PowerPoint presentations. Slides are also often misused. Slides containing printed material should be kept simple and must be clearly visible from the back of the lecture space with the lights on. Care must be taken when reproducing material from books and journals, as it often contains far too much information. Coloured slides of relevant material and examples are ideal for illustrating points and for adding variety and interest. When using slides, avoid turning off the lights for more than brief periods. The level of attention will rapidly fall, however interesting your slides happen to be!

Computer presentation systems (eg PowerPoint) are rapidly taking over the function performed by both the overhead and slide projector. If you teach in locations where you are confident of the technology to support a computer presentation, then there are many advantages to using this technological aid, including ease and flexibility of preparation and the capacity to generate student notes derived directly from your presentation. You can also incorporate video and sound in your presentation as required. In Chapter 7, we give you more information about preparing and using these systems.

A computer presentation is governed by the same princi-ples as those for slides and overheads – clear, legible text and pictures, and the use of a room where sufficient lighting can be left on for student note taking and activi-ties. If you are not confident of the environment in which you are teaching, it is still wise to have overhead trans-parencies or slide backups in traditional media.

Films and videos are best used in short segments. Their use requires more careful planning, as it will be necessary to have a projectionist if a film is to be shown and probably a technician to set up video equipment. How-ever, the effort is well worthwhile for both the impact of the content and the variety it introduces. We use such material to show illustrative examples and practical tech-niques. Films or videotapes may also be used in attempts to influence attitude or to explore emotionally charged issues. A short segment can be shown illustrating a challenging situation (trigger film), and the class asked to react to this situation. Films and videos for this purpose are commercially available in some disciplines.

Some teachers choose to show a full-length film or video. The educational value of this medium is enhanced if it is carefully integrated into the teaching. This integration can be done by:

● Selecting and previewing the film very carefully.
● During the preview, preparing notes on how you intend to link the film to the course, how you will introduce it and what activity the students might engage in during or after viewing it.
● Using the film in the way you plan and ensuring that you have ample time for all the viewing and related activities.

If you believe that a film is particularly important, you can enhance its value by showing it twice: first to introduce students to it and second to focus attention (through the use of prepared questions or tasks) on specific matters of importance.

WHEN THINGS GO WRONG

Throughout this book, we present the view that things are less likely to go 'wrong' if you have carefully prepared yourself for the teaching task. However, unexpected difficulties can and do arise, so strategies to deal with these need to be part of your teaching skills. In our experience, problems in teaching large groups are likely to fall into one of the categories listed below.

Problems with audiovisual material and equipment. An equipment failure can be a potential disaster if you have prepared a computer presentation or a series of slides for projection. Preventive measures include having a thorough understanding of your equipment, back-up equipment to hand, and learning to change blown bulbs or remove jammed slides.

If these measures are to no avail, you will have to continue without the materials and may do so successfully, provided that you have taken care to have a clear record in your notes of the content of your material. Photocopied enlargements of slides of data are a useful back-up here. Using these, you may be able to present some of the information verbally, on a whiteboard or on an overhead transparency if the original problem was with the slide projector. You will not, of course, be able to use this approach with illustrations and you may have to substitute careful description and perhaps blackboard sketches to cover essential material. Whatever you do, do not pass around your materials as they may be damaged. Also, by the time most members of the audience receive them, they will no longer be directly relevant to what you are saying!

Difficulties with your presentation. Losing your place and running out of time can be disconcerting. If this should happen, do not start apologizing or communicating your sense of 'panic'. Instead, pause, calmly evaluate your situation, decide on a course of action and continue. One lecturer we know simply invites students to check their notes while she simply cleans the board as she thinks through what to do next!

Challenges from students. We have deliberately avoided the use of the word 'problem' in relation to your interaction with students because the 'problem' may be with you (your manner, your preparation or presentation, for example) or it could be in the form of a genuinely motivated intellectual challenge to what you have been doing or saying. It is essential to be clear as to exactly *what* the challenge is and *why* it has occurred before you act.

Many teachers fear confrontation with students in a class. We cannot go into all aspects of classroom management and discipline here, but we can identify a number of principles and refer you to more detailed discussions elsewhere (McKeachie's *Teaching Tips* is a useful reference).

Disruptive behaviour and talking in class are common challenges and must not be ignored, both for the sake of your own concentration and for the majority of students who are there to learn. Simply stopping talking and waiting patiently for quiet usually overcomes minor disturbances. If this happens more than once, the other students will usually make their displeasure known to the offenders. If the disruption is more serious, you will have to speak directly to the students concerned and indicate that you are aware of the offence. But do initially try to treat it with humour or you may alienate the rest of the class. If the problem persists, indicate that you will be unable to tolerate the situation again and that you will have to ask them to leave. Make sure you do just this if the problem re-emerges. Do so firmly and calmly. If the situation leads to confrontation, it is probably best if you leave the room. It is remarkable what effect this has on students! Make every attempt to meet the offenders afterwards to deal with the problem.

We have been appalled at accounts of teachers who endure the most unreasonable physical and verbal abuse in classes and do nothing about it – other than suffer inwardly. There is no need for this and the majority of students will look for firm but fair disciplinary measures. An added measure is to arrange arriving and leaving classes so that you have time to get to know at least some of the students in the class – especially potentially troublesome ones. The active-learning strategies we have suggested in this chapter are also ways of addressing these challenges – both by engaging students in their own learning (and using up some of their energy in that way!) and giving you a further opportunity to get to know them. Anonymity is a great accomplice in disruptive behaviour!

EVALUATING LARGE-GROUP TEACHING

Improving the quality of your teaching in large groups will depend on a combination of experience and your willingness to critically evaluate your performance. Evaluation may be seen as informal or formal. The informal way may involve asking several students whom you know for their comments. It may also be undertaken by asking yourself a series of questions immediately after your teaching, such as:

- How much time was taken to prepare?
- Were the notes helpful?
- Were the visual aids clear and easy to read?
- What steps could be taken to improve preparation and organization of the active-learning tasks?
- Did the questions stimulate discussion?
- What did I learn about students' understanding from their questions/comments/written responses to the CATs?
- Were the purposes of the session achieved? How do I know this?

The distribution of questionnaires to the class is a more formal way of evaluating teaching. Many such forms have been designed and can usually be obtained from the teaching unit within your institution. An example of such a form developed and tested by one of us is included at the end of the chapter. The questions asked have been derived from research on effective teaching. However, like all such forms, its main limitation is that it cannot present answers to all the questions you may think are relevant. Accordingly, you should consider adding to or adapting such forms to your own special needs. The best way of obtaining an independent evaluation is to seek the services of a teaching unit. They will sit in on your teaching, prepare a detailed analysis and go over it with you later.

A CONCLUDING THOUGHT – IF YOU MUST 'LECTURE'...

It may be objected that the crowded curriculum does not allow time for the active-learning techniques described in this chapter. This objection rests on the argument that material has to be 'covered'. However, it also assumes that students will learn that material. This is unfortunately not usually the case, as we have already shown that levels of attention to a traditional expository lecture decline, and it is known that other indicators of performance such as recall and even pulse rates fall fairly rapidly around 20 minutes after the lecture begins. Worse, what little is learnt in the remainder of the lecture time interferes with understanding earlier material.

So, if you feel the inclination to 'lecture' in order to cover the material, perhaps the question you should be asking yourself is 'Should I be wasting so much time speaking for 50 minutes?'. In some courses, it is the case that a few students regard lectures as an important learning activity. Further, lectures are perceived as being a means to pace study, a way of keeping in touch with coursework, and as supplementary to other more important learning activities such as practical classes, tutorials and assignments. At worst, lectures are seen as a boring waste of time relieved only by the skill and daring of the paper-plane throwers and other attention seekers!

The challenge is to work out a clear and educationally defensible rationale for lecturing. Lecturing can only be a useful *learning* method for students where the techniques of teaching large groups are appropriately employed. We hope that this chapter has contributed to dealing with these challenges.

GUIDED READING

Almost all books that are concerned with the practicalities of teaching in higher education will devote some space to the lecture method of teaching large numbers of students and you will undoubtedly find many of these helpful.

Perhaps the most popular book on lecturing is Donald Bligh's *What's the Use of Lectures?*. Bligh's book gives an overview of the research on this subject, provides useful information on preparing and delivering lectures and has an interesting section on alternatives to the lecture. Most libraries will have the first edition of this book, published by Penguin in 1972. However, a recent 1998 fifth edition is available from the publisher, Intellect, at the address below:

Intellect,
School of Art and Design,
Earl Richards Road North,
Exeter, EX2 6AS
UK

There are several well-written books that give practical advice. A recommended one is George Brown's *Lecturing and Explaining* (Methuen, London, 1978). This book is full of exercises and suggested activities that you can carry out for yourself or with a colleague. Another is *Lecturing* by Robert Cannon (HERDSA Green Guide, No 7, 1992). This provides more detail than is provided in this chapter on preparation, presentation, evaluation and active-learning methods. It is available from the Higher Education Research and Development Society of Australasia at the address below:

HERDSA
PO Box 516
Jamieson ACT 2614
Australia

Another useful book that reviews ideas on improving learning from lectures is *53 Interesting Things to Do in Your Lectures* by G Gibbs, S Habeshaw and T Habeshaw (Technical and Educational Services Ltd, Bristol, 1992). There is also a large amount of published literature on active learning in large groups. A good introduction to this concept is *Promoting Active Learning* by Chet Meyers and Thomas Jones (Jossey-Bass, San Francisco, 1993).

Books and journals referred to in this chapter

Angelo, T A and Cross, K P (1993) *Classroom Assessment Techniques: A handbook for college teachers*, Jossey Bass, San Francisco.

Buzan, T (1988) *Make the Most of Your Mind*, Pan, London.

McKeachie, W J (1994) *Teaching Tips: Strategies, research, and theory for college and university*, 9th edn, DC Heath, Toronto.

Overall, Christine (1998) 'Feeling fraudulent', in *A Feminist I: Reflections from academia*, Chapter 6, Broadview Press, Peterborough, Ontario.

Ware, J E and Williams, R G (1975) 'The Doctor Fox Effect: A study of lecturer effectiveness and rating of instruction', *Journal of Medical Education*, **50**, pp 149–156.

The University of Adelaide
Advisory Centre for University Education

Student Evaluation of Teaching

in

UNIVERSITY EDUCATION

Semester 1, 2000

This questionnaire seeks information about your experiences of this subject. Please circle the number which most closely corresponds to your own view about each statement. If you feel that you cannot answer a particular question, circle the 'Not Applicable' category. Your responses are anonymous. However, be aware that this questionnaire will be returned to the teacher after being analysed by the ACUE. Therefore, print your comments to preserve your anonymity.

Teacher: A/Prof. R. CANNON

	Outstanding						Very Poor	Not Applicable
1. All things considered, how would you rate this person's effectiveness as a university teacher?	7	6	5	4	3	2	1	X

	Strongly Agree			Undecided		Strongly Disagree		Not Applicable
2. Communicated effectively	7	6	5	4	3	2	1	X
3. Taught in a way that made note-taking easy	7	6	5	4	3	2	1	X
4. Was enthusiastic	7	6	5	4	3	2	1	X
5. Was interested in helping students to learn	7	6	5	4	3	2	1	X
6. Was accessible to students seeking advice	7	6	5	4	3	2	1	X
7. Encouraged students to express ideas	7	6	5	4	3	2	1	X
8. Was well organised	7	6	5	4	3	2	1	X
9. Was confident	7	6	5	4	3	2	1	X
10. Gave clear explanations	7	6	5	4	3	2	1	X

11. What were the best aspects of this person's teaching? *(print your comments)*

The Subject

	Strongly Agree		Undecided		Strongly Disagree		Not Applicable
12. I am happy with the content of this course	7	6	5	4	3	2	1	X

	Very Heavy		Reasonable		Very Light		Not Applicable
13. Overall, the workload for this course was	7	6	5	4	3	2	1	X

	Strongly Agree		Undecided		Strongly Disagree		Not Applicable
14. The pace was too slow	7	6	5	4	3	2	1	X

	Very Difficult		Reasonable		Very Easy		Not Applicable
15. In terms of difficulty, the subject matter was	7	6	5	4	3	2	1	X

	Strongly Agree		Undecided		Strongly Disagree		Not Applicable
16. I understood the subject matter presented	7	6	5	4	3	2	1	X
17. The course was well coordinated	7	6	5	4	3	2	1	X
18. The course was challenging	7	6	5	4	3	2	1	X
19. Assessment methods were fair	7	6	5	4	3	2	1	X
20. Course handouts were well prepared	7	6	5	4	3	2	1	X
21. The aims of the course were implemented	7	6	5	4	3	2	1	X
22. The course has been a worthwhile learning experience . .	7	6	5	4	3	2	1	X
23. The recommended readings were valuable for my understanding of the course	7	6	5	4	3	2	1	X
24. The course stimulated my interest in the subject	7	6	5	4	3	2	1	X

25. In what ways could this course be improved? *(print your comments)*

Chapter 5 Making a Presentation at a Conference

INTRODUCTION

This chapter may appear to be out of place in a book about education and teaching. However, most teachers, at some time, will wish to make a presentation at a conference or professional meeting, and there are many obvious similarities between large group teaching and presenting a paper. There are also significant differences which may not be quite so obvious which made us feel that this chapter might be appreciated.

Poster sessions are popular at many national and international meetings as an alternative to the formal presentation of papers. We have, therefore, included a short section on the preparation of a conference poster.

In due course, you will be asked to take on the responsibility of chairing a conference session. This also has its pitfalls so a section on this topic concludes the chapter.

PRESENTING A PAPER

Though much of the advice given in the chapter on large group teaching is just as relevant in this section, the aims of a meeting or conference are different enough to warrant separate consideration. Much of this relates to the imposition of a strict time limit. If you are in the position to give a paper it is certain that you will have a lot to say, far more in fact than can possibly be delivered in the time allocated. You will also be caught in the difficult situation of many of the audience being unfamiliar with the details of your area of interest, some of the audience knowing considerably more than you do about the area, and all of the audience likely to be critical of the content and the presentation. These and other factors make the giving of a paper a pressure situation, particularly for the young and inexperienced hoping to make a good impression on peers and superiors. However, it is also a situation that is amenable to resolution by careful planning and attention to technique.

PREPARING THE PAPER

There are three stages that you must go through during the preparation of a conference paper. These stages are:

- the collection and selection of information and data;
- the arrangement (getting the structure right and deciding on the most suitable presentation);
- polishing, writing it out and rehearsal.

The collection and selection of the data

There is a great tendency for speakers to cram more than is possible into their papers with the inevitable consequence of either speaking too fast or going over time. The audience is primarily interested in hearing a short, cohesive account of your ideas or research. To achieve this you are not going to be able to present all your hard-won data. You will have to be very selective and in most instances you will have to restrict yourself to only one aspect of your work. Your first step should be to write down in one sentence the main purpose of your paper. In other words, what is the main message you wish to get across? Having done this you should identify the three or four pieces of evidence you will use to give support to your views. You should keep in mind that you will only have two or three minutes to describe each piece of work so that when you are assembling your data you must be aware of the need to simplify the results into a more easily digested form (eg complex tables reconstructed into histograms).

The arrangement

The first task is to get the basic plan worked out. The presentation will fall into several components. For a research paper, a basic plan might look like this:

- Introduction.
- Statement of the purpose of your research.
- Description of methods and results.
- Conclusions.

The introduction: This is a vital component. It must set the context of your work for the audience, many of whom may not be experts in your field. They may also be suffering the after-effects of the previous paper or of a dash from another concurrent session venue. You have no more than two minutes to excite the interest of the audience before they relapse into the mental torpor so prevalent at conferences. You must therefore give a considerable amount of thought to the introduction. It must be simple, precise and free from jargon. It must start from a broad base so that the audience can identify the point at which your research fits into the discipline and make them appreciate the vital importance of your own contribution.

The statement of purpose: This should take no more than a minute but it is also a critical component of the talk. In these few sentences you will need to convince the audience that what you set out to do was worthwhile. It should flow from the introduction so that it sounds like a logical outcome of previous research.

The description of methods and results: The description of methods will usually have to be abbreviated or even reduced to a mention ('The so-and-so technique was used to…'). If the development of a new method is an important part of your work then it must obviously be described in more detail but you must decide whether the main message is to relate to the method or the results subsequently obtained.

The results are usually the most important part of the paper. You will inevitably have spent a lot of time getting them together. It is possible that you have already prepared a variety of tables, graphs and charts for the purpose of publication. Do not fall into the trap of thinking that these are suitable for presentation to a live audience. How often have you, for example, sat in a meeting where someone has projected slides of an incomprehensible and illegible table or a wall of prose taken straight from a journal?

The conclusions: These must flow naturally from the results of your work. You will aim to make one or two clear statements that you can conclude from your work. It is advisable to be reasonably modest in your claims.

The presentation aids

The second task is to prepare the visual aids, and possibly handouts, to support your paper. In most instances these will be slides, overhead transparencies or a computer-based presentation. Considerable thought must be given to these as their impact and quality may make or break the presentation. They must complement your oral presentation, not duplicate it. The technical aspects of the preparation of slides and overhead transparencies are covered in greater detail in Chapter 7, which deals with teaching aids, but a few specific points are worth mentioning at this time.

Having roughed out the plan of the talk it should be reasonably obvious where a slide (or transparency) is required. You may need one or two during the introduction to stimulate interest.

The slides or overheads of the results provide you with the greatest challenge. It is during this part of your paper that the visual material will often be of more importance than the verbal ('A picture says a thousand words'). Avoid complex tables and where possible convert tables to charts or simple graphs. Rarely is it appropriate to show masses of data; just show the mean or rounded-off figures. If you feel you really must refer to complex data it is better to have this prepared in printed form and available to the audience as a handout.

Having prepared the visual aids, check that they are accurate and legible. (As a rule, a slide where the information can be read with the naked eye will be satisafactory when projected. Lettering on an overhead transparency must be no less than 5 mm high and for a computer-based presentation, a minimum of 32 points is suggested). Then take them to a large lecture theatre and project them. Check that they are indeed legible from the furthermost corners of the theatre. It is also helpful to take a colleague with you to check that the message is clear and that there are no spelling mistakes.

Polishing, writing it out and rehearsal

At this stage you should have a good idea of what you intend to say and of the aids that you require. It is now advisable to write the text of the talk in full. Do not write in the style you use for journal publications. Pretend you are talking to an individual and write in a conversational mode, avoiding jargon wherever possible.

As you go along, identify the correct position for the aids. As you do this you may find places where you have not prepared an appropriate slide or overhead. Remember, during the talk the visual aids and handouts must complement your talk and not distract from it. There must always be an accurate match between the content of your aids and what you are saying. When using slides, if you do not have one which illustrates what you are saying, insert a blank slide. This will also avoid the distracting practice of saying 'slide-off' and 'slide-on'. If you intend to use the same slide more than once in your presentation, make copies to avoid the confusion that will ensue if you ask the projectionist to go back to a previous slide.

Once you have the rough draft, edit it. Then read it aloud at about the pace you think you will go during the presentation. Further editing and alterations will be required, as almost certainly you will have gone over time. Some find it a useful strategy to record the talk on a tape-recorder and listen to the result very critically.

The next stage is to present the paper to an honest and critical colleague. The feedback is often extremely valuable.

You must now decide whether you will read the paper or not. Most authorities consider that you should be well enough rehearsed to speak only with the aid of cue cards or the cues provided by your slides. If you have a highly visual presentation most of the audience will be looking at the screen so the fact that you are reading is less critical. Providing the text is written in a conversational style, and you are able to look up from your text at frequent intervals, then reading is not a major sin. The chief risk of speaking without a text in a very short presentation is going over time which, at best will irritate the chair of your sessions and the audience and, at worst, will result in your being cut-off in mid-sentence.

Rehearsal is essential and a full presentation in front of an audience (eg your department) a week or two before the event is invaluable. Not only will you receive comments on the presentation but you will also be subject to questions, the answering of which, in a precise manner, is just as important as the talk itself. Remember that the quality of your material and its presentation is a public reflection of the quality of your department and institution.

PREPARING THE ABSTRACT AND YOUR CONTRIBUTION TO THE PROCEEDINGS OF THE CONFERENCE

The abstract

Most conferences will require you to prepare an abstract, sometimes several months before the meeting. Initially, it may be used to help select contributions and, ultimately, will be made available to participants. Contributors are often tardy in preparing their abstracts which is discourteous to the conference organizers and makes their task more difficult.

The abstract should be an advertisement for your paper. It should outline the background to the study and summarize the supporting data and the main conclusions. Quite frequently, abstracts promise what they do not deliver so avoid being guilty of false advertising.

The proceedings

Many national and most major international conferences will publish proceedings. Should you be presenting a paper at such a conference you will be required to provide your contribution to these proceedings during the conference or shortly afterwards. It is not appropriate to present the organizers with the script and slides that you have just used in your presentation. The contribution to the proceedings should be written in a style consistent with that used in a journal article. The content should be the same as in the presented paper but not necessarily identical. It is perfectly permissible to expand some areas, particularly with regard to the methods and results sections, where more detail could be included. This should all be done within the guidelines for format and length specified by the organizers.

WHAT YOU SHOULD DO ON THE DAY

'There's many a slip 'twixt cup and lip.' This saying provides a reminder that, however good your preparation for the presentation of the paper has been, there is still plenty that can happen to ruin your carefully laid plans. Fortunately, many such problems can be prevented or anticipated. You should find it helpful to work your way through the checklist shown in Figure 5.1.

FIGURE 5.1 CHECKLIST TO USE ON THE DAY OF THE PRESENTATION

Before the presentation

- Check your slides and overheads to see that they are in the correct order, labelled in this order and, if slides are used, spotted in the correct place (see Figure 7.4 on page 128).
- Load your slides, or boot up your computer slide show. Project them to check they are in the right order and to be sure that you can operate the equipment correctly and confidently.
- Seek out the technician and explain your plan for the projection and the arrangements for lighting.
- Check your prompt cards or text.
- Check the venue and the operation of the computer, slide or overhead projector. You may be expected to operate the lights, a computer, a slide changer or a light pointer. Have a practice during a break in the programme.
- If you are expected to use a microphone check how it is attached and adjusted.
- Try and sit in on a talk in the same venue early in the day to get a feel for the acoustics and how you should use the audiovisual facilities.

During the presentation

- Walk confidently to the podium and arrange your cards or text. Adjust the microphone and set out the position of pointers, overhead transparencies, slide changers and so on to your satisfaction.
- Commence your talk with an appropriate opening (eg 'Madam President, Mr Chairman, ladies and gentlemen').
- Present the opening few sentences without reference to any notes, looking around the audience without fixing your eye on any particular individual, however friendly or prestigious that person may be.
- Call for the lights to be dimmed (or do it yourself) when your first slide is to appear. Never turn off the lights completely unless it is absolutely essential and in any case only for a minimum of time. On the other hand do not continually call for 'lights on' or 'lights off'. Your slides should have been designed to be clearly visible in subdued light.
- Speak at a rate which sounds slow to you – it will not be too slow for the audience. Try and use more emphasis than seems natural to your own ear – again, it will not sound too theatrical to the audience. Let your enthusiasm show through by using suitable hand and facial gestures.
- If you turn to the screen to point something out make sure you do not move away from the microphone. This is a particular problem with a fixed microphone, in which case move behind it so that you continue to speak across it.
- When you come to the conclusion, say so ('In conclusion I have shown...' or 'Finally,...').

Handling questions

Most conferences have a fixed period of time for questions. In some ways this is the most critical part of the presentation. Some people in the audience may test you out with penetrating questions and how you handle them will enhance or detract from the impact of your performance. This is one of the reasons why we suggested a full rehearsal in front of your department in order to practise your answering of difficult questions and to avoid leaving weaknesses in your arguments for which some participants may be searching. Figure 5.2 lists some points to remember.

FIGURE 5.2 *POINTS TO REMEMBER WHEN HANDLING QUESTIONS*

- Listen to the question very carefully.
- If the question is complex or if you have any concern that not all the audience heard it, restate it clearly and succinctly.
- Answer the question politely and precisely. Sometimes a simple 'yes' or 'no' will be sufficient. Avoid the danger of using the question to give what amounts to a second paper.
- Be alert to the questioners who are deliberately trying to trick you or to use the occasion to display their own knowledge of the subject.
- If the question is particularly awkward or aggressive try to deflect it as best you can. Strategies include agreeing with as much of what was said as possible, acknowledging legitimate differences of opinion or interpretation, or suggesting you meet the questioner afterwards to clarify your position. At all costs avoid a dispute in front of your audience. However, do not be afraid to politely disagree with any questioners, however eminent, when you are sure of your ground. Remember, they may only be testing you out!

PREPARING A CONFERENCE POSTER

The conference poster is a popular alternative to presenting papers at conferences. You will find that the

poster has several advantages over the traditional paper such as:

- allowing readers to consider material at their own rate;
- being available for viewing over an extended period of time;
- enabling participants to engage in more detailed discussion with the presenter than is the case with the usually rushed paper discussion session.

If the conference organizers have arranged a poster session we suggest that you consider taking advantage of it. It may provide you with an opportunity to present additional material to the conference that would otherwise be difficult because of limitations on the number of speakers.

What is a conference poster?

A conference poster is a means of presenting information on a static display. A poster should include at least the following parts:

- a title;
- an abstract;
- text and diagrams;
- name of author(s), their address(es) and where they may be contacted during the conference.

Additional materials that you might consider for the poster, or in support of the poster, include:

- illustrations;
- exhibits and objects;
- audiovisual displays;
- a take-away handout, which might be a printed reduction of your poster;
- a blank pad, so that when you are not in attendance, interested readers can leave comments or contact addresses for you to follow-up.

Preparing the poster

If you decide that a poster is an appropriate way of presenting your information, there are a number of things you must take into consideration during its preparation.

Firstly, ascertain from the conference organizers the facilities that will be available. Then proceed to plan the poster. The poster should communicate your message as simply as possible, so do not allow it to become clogged with too much detail. Layout ideas can be gleaned by looking through newspapers and magazines or, better still, from graphic design books and journals. If possible, discuss these ideas with a graphic artist. The layout should be clear, logical and suitable for the material being presented. Try a number of different rough layouts first and seek the opinion of a colleague to determine the best. A possible layout is shown in Figure 5.3.

FIGURE 5.3   POSSIBLE LAYOUT FOR A CONFERENCE POSTER

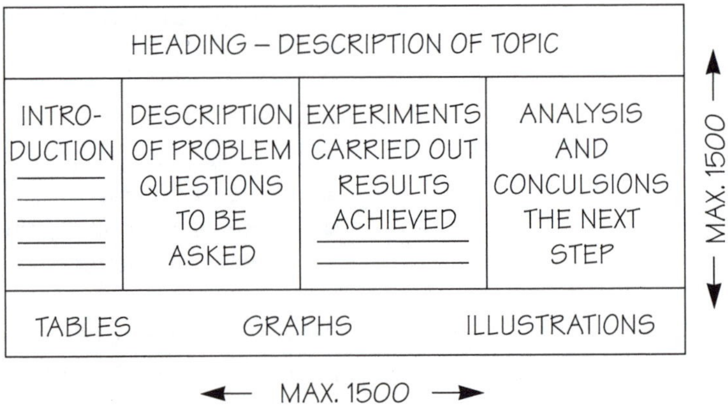

Text lettering should be large enough to be read at the viewing distance, which is likely to be about one metre. In this case, we suggest that the smallest letters be at least 5 mm high and preferably larger. Make sure that diagrams are bold enough to be seen easily and consider using colour to highlight significant points.

Break up the density of text into several discrete parts. For example, consider dividing the text into an abstract, an introduction, a statement of method, results and conclusion – each with its own clear heading. A short list of references or of publications arising out of your work might also be appropriate. Remember that in preparing your poster you are really trying to achieve many of the same things you would wish to achieve with a talk or lecture: to attract attention, maintain interest and to generally communicate effectively.

CHAIRING A CONFERENCE SESSION

Much of the success of a conference will depend on the quality of the chairing of individual sessions. Should this task fall to you there are many responsibilities to fulfil. There are three categories of task – responsibilities to the organizers, to the speaker and to the audience.

Responsibilities to the organizers

The organizers of the conference will have approached you several months before the event. If you are lucky, they will also have given you detailed guidelines to follow but, if not, you must, at a minimum, find out:

- the time and length of the session;
- the number, names and addresses of the speakers;
- a copy of the instructions given to speakers, with particular reference to the time allocated for the presentation and the time allocated for discussion;
- whether there are concurrent sessions.

Ideally, you will contact the speakers in advance of the conference to ensure they have indeed received instructions and understand the implications, particularly with regard to time. You may find that some are inexperienced and nervous about the prospect of their presentation and your advice will be appreciated. Referring the speaker to the earlier parts of this chapter might be valuable.

If early contact has not been made, it is essential to meet with speakers before the session. You must clarify the format of the session and reinforce your intention to stick rigidly to the allocated time. You should explain the method to be used to indicate when there is one minute to go, when time is up and what steps you will take should the speaker continue for longer. This may sound draconian but, believe us, it is vital. A timing device on the lectern is an invaluable aid to compliance.

Before the session, you must also familiarize yourself with the layout of the venue, the audiovisual facilities and the lighting. In the absence of a technician, you may be called on to operate the equipment and lighting or to instruct the speakers in their use.

At the start of the session, announce that you intend to keep to time – and do so.

Finally, you must be certain that the session and individual presentations commence and finish at the programmed time. This is particularly important when there are concurrent sessions.

Responsibilities to the speakers

Speakers invariably fall into one of three categories:

The well-organized speakers: These will tell you exactly what they are going to do and what they require. If you ask them how long they are going to speak, they will tell you in minutes and seconds! You will need to have little concern for these speakers, but they will expect you to be as well-prepared and organized as themselves.

The apprehensive speakers: These will generally be younger and less experienced. They will often have a well-prepared paper to present but are in danger of not doing themselves justice. You can assist such speakers greatly by familiarizing them with the facilities before the session and encouraging them to practise operating the audio-visual equipment. If this seems beyond them, you may be able to take on the task yourself. Calm reassurance that all will be well is the message to convey.

The confident under-prepared speaker: These are remarkably prevalent and the most dangerous for the chairperson. They will not seek advice and will deny having received detailed instructions about their presentation. When you ask them how long they expect to speak, you will receive an offhand response. This will tell you that they have not rehearsed their presentation and will almost certainly go over time. There is little you can do to help such people because they are certain that they have everything under control. However, they can be your downfall unless you prepare to intervene. Before the session you must convince them that you are serious about cutting them off if they speak over time. Unfortunately, this strategy will often fail and you must be prepared to act immediately the first time a speaker goes over the allotted time. After a maximum of 15 seconds grace, rise from your chair. If the hint is not immediately taken, you have no option but to politely but firmly stop the speaker. Examples can be cited of such speakers being physically led off the stage still talking, but such extremes should not arise! Fortunately, you will only have to intervene in such a way once in a session and, should it happen, your future as an invited chairperson is assured.

In the discussion period you must see fair play. Ensure that questions are relevant and brief. Do not allow questioners to make long statements or commence a minipresentation of their own work. Suggest that any significant differences of opinion be explored informally at the subsequent coffee-break.

Responsibilities to the audience

The audience has a right to expect several things from the chairperson. They must be able to hear the speaker and see the slides. They must be reassured that you will keep the speakers to time to protect their opportunity to ask questions and to allow them to move to subsequent sessions. Speakers going over time is the commonest complaint of participants and the chairperson is usually held to blame. During the question period you should ensure that the time is not monopolized by the intellectual heavies in the front rows. On the other hand you must also be well prepared to ask the first question if none is immediately forthcoming from the audience.

Finishing off

At the close of the session, thank the speakers and the audience. Also remind them of the starting time of the next session. You may also have been asked to transmit information from the organizers. Particularly important would be to obtain completed evaluation forms for the session if these were provided.

GUIDED READING

A classic book we can still recommend for further reading on scientific presentations is Calnan and Barabas' *Speaking at Medical Meetings* (Heinemann, London, 1972). This pocket-sized do-it-yourself guide is not only valuable but entertaining. It contains many useful illustrations and good advice.

An excellent general text on public speaking is C Turk's *Effective Speaking* (Spon, London, 1985). This is a comprehensive reference work that has been written by a university lecturer. You should consider obtaining a copy for your personal library.

Another very comprehensive resource is Stephen Lucas' *The Art of Public Speaking* (McGraw-Hill, New York, 1995).

The references at the end of Chapter 7 will provide further guidance on preparing visual material for conferences.

Chapter 6   Teaching Practical and Laboratory Classes

INTRODUCTION

Practical and laboratory classes are usually regarded as essential components of science and technology-based courses. They are also found in some arts-related disciplines (eg geography, languages, psychology). In this chapter, we will try to identify those objectives that are best achieved in practical classes and discuss the ways in which you can assist your students to achieve them. This is important, as studies have shown that student reactions to practical work are variable. There are several possible reasons for this. One significant reason may be that the running of practical classes is often left to junior staff who may not have the experience or authority to recognize and rectify deficiencies. This is often not their fault, as staff training in laboratory class supervision is rarely provided. Designing, implementing and running a practical course is a complex, and expensive, component of the curriculum requiring the skill and support of senior staff.

To make the best use of resources available for practical work we strongly suggest you obtain a copy of *Improving Teaching and Learning in Laboratories* by Hazel and Baillie, upon which we have drawn liberally for the material in this chapter. We would also recommend obtaining the video cited at the end of the chapter, which illustrates case studies from a range of disciplines.

THE ATTRIBUTES OF AN EFFECTIVE PRACTICAL-CLASS TEACHER

These have been identified on the bases of the opinions of experts, the perceptions of students, and from observations of actual teaching. As the role of the teacher seems to be particularly critical in the laboratory setting if the aims of such courses are to be achieved, you may find it salutary to check yourself against these attributes:

- Do you encourage active participation by students and avoid having them stand around in an observational capacity?
- Do you have and demonstrate a positive attitude to your teaching?
- Is the emphasis of your teaching on critical thinking, problem solving, aspects of scientific enquiry and other intellectual activities that require the students to think?
- Do you encourage students to focus on the integration of the practical exercises with the learning material taught in other components of the course?
- Do you supervise students closely enough to recognize those having difficulties with the concepts on which the exercises are based?
- Do you provide adequate opportunities for your students to practise their skills?
- Do you provide a good role model?
- Does your teaching provide stimulation and challenge?
- Are you friendly, helpful and available to your students?

Should your honest answer to some of these questions be 'no', then you are probably a typical teacher, for research has shown that these desirable attributes are rarely all present. Just being aware of these attributes should encourage you to be more critical of your approach.

The remainder of this chapter will deal with some methods that could enhance your effectiveness when teaching in the laboratory or other practical situations.

THE PURPOSES OF PRACTICAL AND LABORATORY TEACHING

The purpose of practical and laboratory classes will vary somewhat depending on whether the course is primarily for students of the discipline (eg chemistry for chemistry students) or is a service course for another department or faculty (eg chemistry for engineering students). If you are teaching students of your own faculty, the emphasis will be on the fundamentals of the discipline. Not surprisingly perhaps, most teachers will find it easier to relate to this situation than to adapt to service-course teaching where the expectation is to teach only those aspects of the discipline which are relevant to the client department or faculty. Teachers may feel less motivated to carry out this task, with potential serious consequences for the students. If you find yourself in such a situation, you must liaise with your colleagues from the client area and attempt to get an understanding of their specific needs. If you take the trouble to do so, you may find it is a more interesting and challenging experience than you had anticipated.

There are many and varied potential objectives for practical teaching, including learning scientific knowledge and concepts, developing creativity, attaining professional values, learning to work cooperatively and so on. However, in an area in which there is an increasing concern about cost containment, there are alternative instructional strategies which may achieve such objectives as effectively and more efficiently. The only two objectives that can be said to be best achieved in the laboratory setting are:

- learning practical skills and techniques relevant to the discipline; and
- understanding the process of scientific enquiry.

Learning practical skills and techniques

The laboratory is the place where organized opportunities can be provided for students to appreciate and practise a range of skills and techniques that someone graduating from the course would be expected to have acquired. These basic skills and techniques should be defined so that students have a clear idea of what is expected. Such skills are best stated in terms of what the student should have achieved by the end of the course (these statements are known as 'behavioural objectives'). An example might be: 'At the end of the class, the student will be expected to set up and operate a [particular piece of equipment]'.

Understanding the process of scientific enquiry

This is obviously something fundamental to the teaching of science and, clearly, the practical class is potentially one of the most valuable opportunities for the students to acquire such an understanding. Yet research has consistently shown that many courses that espouse this purpose fail dismally in its achievement. The reasons for this are many, but include a lack of planning and inappropriate teaching strategies. It is important to clarify what the process of scientific enquiry means in your discipline and what activities can be performed by students to enable them to develop the necessary insights and skills. The general headings are likely to include the following:

- critical analysis of literature;
- identification of and grappling with set or novel problems;
- analysis and interpretation of experimental data;
- written and verbal communication.

COURSE PLAN AND TEACHING METHODS

It is to be hoped that the practical classes are well integrated into an overall course plan and that this is readily available to you and to the students. Unfortunately, this is not always the case. If a plan is not available, you should try to generate one using the procedures suggested in Chapter 8 on curriculum planning. It is helpful to have a plan that identifies the aims of the course and from which you can identify the aims that are to be achieved in the practical classes as opposed to lectures and tutorials. When this is done, you may find that the current classes are not meeting the expected objectives either in breadth or in depth. This is because many practical courses have evolved over time in an *ad hoc* way rather than being planned or constantly upgraded on the basis of course evaluation.

The assessment of **breadth** will come from having a defined series of topics and skills, which the students are expected to cover and acquire. The assessment of **depth** is more difficult and requires an honest and critical appraisal of the content of the laboratory exercises. This may reveal that the intellectual effort required by the student is about the same as following a recipe in a cookbook while you were hoping that they were attaining skills in the process of scientific enquiry. In their book, Hazel and Baillie classify laboratory activities into three types, depending on their purpose:

- controlled exercises and demonstrations;
- experimental investigations; and
- research projects.

Controlled exercises and demonstrations

These are exercises wholly devised by staff. The main purpose is to help students to develop fundamental skills and techniques that have to be mastered. Demonstrations have a useful role in introducing students to important concepts and showing features of a piece of equipment. For a demonstration to be effective, all students must be able to see and appreciate what is going on and should find it to be at least interesting and preferably exciting or challenging.

Controlled exercises are most appropriate early in a course when new skills must be acquired before more advanced work can be undertaken. You must be alert to the ever-present danger that such exercises lead to students simply following a series of instructions and becoming bored. Under such circumstances, learning will be minimal. The basic *procedure* to follow when conducting a controlled exercise is shown in Figure 6.1. For an *example* of such a controlled exercise, see Figure 6.2.

FIGURE 6.1   PROCEDURE FOR CONDUCTING A CONTROLLED EXERCISE

Procedure

- Define the objectives of the exercise ('At the end of the class you will be able to…')
- Identify reading material to be given to students before the class.
- Provide a detailed account of the procedure to be followed by students.
- Identify and provide all laboratory materials and equipment.
- Specify the observations that have to be made.
- Describe the nature of the report required for assessment purposes.

Experimental investigations

The principal characteristic of this type of exercise is the provision of an opportunity for students to display some initiative and exert an element of choice in the design and conduct of the experimental work. The idea is to simulate, albeit still in a controlled and limited way, the process of scientific enquiry. The problems selected should be a natural extension of the students' previous understanding and experience. Such an activity could proceed over several classes. It might aim to relate only to one aspect of the process of scientific enquiry. For example, the students might be provided with a novel problem and asked to generate a series of possible hypotheses and experiments without any expectations that the experiments would ever be performed. On the other hand, students could be provided with experimental data and asked to analyse and interpret these even though they had not themselves performed the experiments. Generally speaking, some practical work will be involved over which the student has some degree of choice and control (see Figure 6.3). For an example of an experimental investigation, see Figure 6.4.

FIGURE 6.2   EXAMPLE OF
A CONTROLLED LABORATORY
EXERCISE

OBJECTIVE	REFERENCE MATERIAL	LABORATORY ACTIVITIES
AT THE END OF THIS CLASS THE STUDENT WILL BE ABLE TO COLLECT AND APPROPRIATELY EXAMINE A MID-STREAM SPECIMEN OF URINE (MSU).	LECTURE NOTES AND HANDOUTS; TEXT REFERENCES. DETAILS OF PROCEDURES FOR COLLECTION AND ANALYSIS IN LABORATORY MANUAL.	1. THE PATIENT IS YOU, COLLECT AN MSU. 2. CHECK pH, PROTEIN AND OTHER BIO-CHEMICAL TESTS USING THE DIP STICKS. 3. EXAMINE SPECIMEN MICROSCOPIC-ALLY. 4. PLATE SPECIMEN AND INCUBATE FOR 24 HOURS.

		5. HAVE YOUR TUTOR CHECK YOUR PROCEDURES. 6. RECORD RESULTS.

FIGURE 6.3 PROCEDURE FOR CONDUCTING A CONTROLLED LABORATORY EXERCISE

Procedure

- Define the objectives of the exercise.
- Identify a series of problems which incorporate the subject area of interest.
- Devise a series of research questions of a limited nature (eg 'What is the effect of changing pH and temperature on the growth characteristics of the bacteria provided?').
- Provide of suggest background resource materials.
- Provide the range of equipment and materials necessary to solve the set problem tasks.
- Describe the nature of the report required for assessment purposes.

FIGURE 6.4 EXAMPLE OF AN EXPERIMENTAL INVESTIGATION

OBJECTIVE	CASE STUDY	LABORATORY
AT THE END OF THIS CLASS THE STUDENT WILL BE ABLE TO DIAGNOSE THE CLINICAL PROBLEM USING APPROPRIATE EXAMPLE OF A LABORATORY INVESTIGATION AND TO PROVIDE A REPORT.	A 26 YEARS OLD WOMAN GAVE A HISTORY OF LOWER ABDOMINAL PAIN ASSOCIATED WITH FREQUENCY AND BURNING SENSATION ON MICTURITION. NO PREVIOUS TREATMENT HAD BEEN GIVEN. TEMPERATURE	1. EXAMINE THE URINE PROVIDED AND MAKE A DIAGNOSIS. 2. WRITE OUT THE LABORATORY FORM THAT SHOULD BE SENT TO THE TREATING DOCTOR.

WAS NORMAL. MICROSCOPIC EXAMINATION OF THE URINE REVEALED 160X 10^6 WHITE BLOOD CELLS/LITRE AND NO CASTS. BIOCHEMICAL TESTING SHOWED NO PROTEIN AND NO GLUCOSE.	3. WHAT OTHER MICROBIO-LOGICAL INVESTIGA-TIONS SHOULD BE CONDUCTED BEFORE THE LABORATORY REPORT CAN BE COMPLETED?

Devising such exercises requires considerable skill. It is important to monitor what students are actually doing and to encourage them to reflect on their work in order to be certain that the aims are being met. If done well, such activities will have a strong motivational effect.

If you are supervising large practical classes, you will need the help of tutors and demonstrators. Their skill and commitment will play a critical part in the success of the course. They must be properly prepared for their role. A useful handbook is referenced at the end of this chapter.

Research projects

Research projects have always held an important place in science-based courses, particularly at Masters, Honours and Doctorate levels. There is now a growing appreciation of their value, albeit in a more limited and less technically demanding form, at an earlier phase of tertiary education. Projects should provide the student with a real-life experience of research that is quite different to the more controlled exercises described previously. They are strongly motivational to most students because of the high level of active participation, the close contact with supervisors and research staff, the lower emphasis on assessment and the greater degree of personal responsibility.

Research projects can be undertaken individually, by groups, or by attachment to a research team in which the student accepts responsibility for certain aspects of an established project. Whatever the approach, the role of the supervisor is critical. Should this be your role, the points outlined in Figure 6.5 should be remembered.

FIGURE 6.5   TASKS FOR THE SUPERVISOR OF A RESEARCH PROJECT

> ### Procedure
>
> - Meet with the student and agree on the objectives of the exercise and the problem to be researched.
> - Work out a schedule of work covering the period during which the project is to be conducted, with provisional deadlines for completion of each stage (eg literature review, hypothesis generation and experimental design; experimental work; data analysis; report).
> - Arrange a regular meeting time with students to check progress (remember the task is to guide not direct).
> - Assist the student to prepare the final report or to give the seminar presentation by means of critical discussion and practice (Students could be referred to the appropriate sections in this book!)

Supervisors vary markedly in their commitment and skill. It is recommended that departments using research projects should provide guidelines and training for supervisors. Most institutions now run courses and provide suitable handbooks. Several valuable publications are available that could be used or modified for this purpose (see Guided Reading at the end of this chapter).

ALTERNATIVE METHODS

A combination of modern technology and interest in new teaching techniques has provided alternatives to the

conventional approaches to practical work already discussed. Two that are now well established are computer-based methods and simulations.

Computer-based methods

The wide availability of computers and their everyday use in all areas of science and technology makes their integration into practical courses almost essential. Early in the curriculum, there may be a need to have practical classes to teach students how to use computers. They may then be introduced as tools for data recording and analysis, as well as for report writing and presentations.

In the laboratory setting, computers may be interfaced with other equipment or used to enhance more conventional practical work. For example, a period of hands-on bench work to obtain skill in operating a piece of equipment might be linked to a computer-based exercise that provides experimental data for analysis, which might otherwise have taken the student several hours to acquire from the bench apparatus. This approach cuts out an aspect of laboratory experience which is often very time consuming and boring for both students and teachers, and enables them to proceed more rapidly to some of the other important objectives of the course.

Learning the skills of data analysis and interpretation is often linked to laboratory teaching. With the computer, it is possible to provide students with a wide range of data sets on which they can practice these skills at varying levels of complexity and sophistication.

Increasingly, individual institutions, consortia and commercial organizations are producing high-quality computer-based instructional materials and course management tools. The modern teacher would be well advised to become familiar with what is available in his or her own discipline through sources such as professional associations and journals, national and international databases of teaching resources, and through searching on the Internet.

An important tenet is: don't be too easily seduced by the attractiveness of the package. We would recommend that you think very carefully about the aims of your course and ensure that the computer-based material is relevant and will meet the aims more effectively and more cheaply than an alternative approach. If possible, arrange to test drive the package yourself and, if possible, organize a visit to another institution where it has been in operation for some time.

Simulations

Simulations are playing an increasingly important role in practical teaching for many reasons. Some reflect a need to provide repetitive practice of basic and advanced skills which might not otherwise be readily available, be too complex (eg acquiring of experimental data), too expensive (eg designing and testing architectural structures) or too dangerous (eg trainee medical staff performing operative procedures). The types of simulation also vary widely, ranging from simple drill and practice (eg using equipment; taking blood samples) through to developing interpersonal skills (eg simulating patients for learning communication skills and management games). The computer is, of course, involved in many of the more complex simulations. The increasing sophistication of graphics and virtual reality will ensure a burgeoning industry in the instructional application of computer-based simulations.

ASSESSMENT

The principles for assessing practical work are the same as for any other component of the course and are discussed in detail in Chapter 9. Here, we only wish to draw your attention to some specific issues in assessing practical work. First, it is important to ensure that the method of

assessment matches the objectives. If, for instance, the objective is to learn to use a piece of equipment or develop a new skill, then these must be observed and assessed against criteria of achievement that have previously been agreed. On the other hand, if the objective is to have the student develop some aspect of scientific thinking, then the method must require the student to demonstrate this approach. This many sound self-evident, but laboratory and project reports often fail to measure those aspects of higher-level thinking that practical work is uniquely placed to assess. It is interesting to consider the fact that the highest correlation with high grades is sometimes neatness!

Alternatives to the conventional written report include self and peer assessments, verbal presentations, posters, practical tests, direct observations of performance during the class, computer-administered exercises and tests and portfolio-based assessments. The latter has been traditionally used in art, design and architecture, and is becoming more widely used in other disciplines. The intention is to provide students with an opportunity to collect a file of work accomplished that can be submitted as evidence of achievement. This may include elements required by the teachers as well as materials submitted by the student. Portfolios are extremely valuable when used for providing feedback ('formative' assessment) but their utility for decision-making purposes ('summative' assessment) has yet to be established for both practical and psychometric reasons.

Feedback is an aspect of teaching that is lacking in almost all courses. It is a very common criticism made by students. Student learning will be greatly facilitated by feedback on their performance and every opportunity should be taken to provide this in written form (eg constructive comments on laboratory reports), by group and individual contact with staff or by structured reports of the kind illustrated in Chapter 9 on assessment.

PUTTING IT TOGETHER

A checklist for the development of a laboratory course which you may find helpful is given in Figure 6.6.

FIGURE 6.6   *CHECKLIST FOR DEVELOPING A LABORATORY COURSE*

- What are the overall goals?
- What are the specific aims for the course/class?
- What are the behavioural objectives for the session and are they written down?
- What tasks must students perform?
- What teaching strategies are to be used?
- How is the course to be sequenced?
- What pre-laboratory requirements are there and how are students to achieve them?
- What post-laboratory work is to be required?
- What form of assessment is to be used and what weight will it receive in relation to other components of the course/curriculum?
- How will the course be monitored?

GUIDED READING

A useful and inexpensive book on practical teaching is the one referred to in this chapter, *Improving Teaching and Learning in Laboratories* by E Hazel and C Baillie (HERDSA Gold Guide No 4, 1998). It is available from:

HERDSA,
PO Box 516,
Jamieson ACT 2614
Australia

For a more detailed treatment of the subject, which also provides illustrative examples from many disciplines, we recommend *Teaching in Laboratories* by D Boud, J Dunn and E Hegarty-Hazel (Open University Press, Guildford, 1989) and *The Student Laboratory and the Science*

Curriculum edited by E Hegarty-Hazel (Routledge, London, 1990).

Helpful chapters on laboratory teaching and effective supervision are to be found in the book *Effective Teaching in Higher Education* by G Brown and M Atkins (Routledge, London, 1988).

A practical handbook directed at tutors and demonstrators is *Tutoring and Demonstrating* edited by F Forster D Hounsell and S Thompson (Centre for Teaching, Learning and Assessment at the University of Edinburgh, Edinburgh, 1995).

The video demonstrating case studies in practical teaching mentioned earlier in the chapter is part of a package, *Teaching Matters 3: Practicals* by J McKenzie *et al* (1993). It is obtainable from the Centre for Learning and Teaching at the University of Technology, Sydney, Australia. In addition to the video, the package contains a workbook for use by training supervisors and demonstrators.

Chapter 7   Preparing Learning and Teaching Materials and Using Technology

INTRODUCTION

This chapter has proved to be challenging to write. The reasons for this are not hard to understand – there is now such rapid development in the application of computers and information-communication technologies in higher education that much of what was said yesterday is out-of-date today! On the other hand, it is fair to judge that as one looks around campuses, for much of the time, most teaching can still be described as 'traditional', with student groups of varying sizes meeting with a teacher for a set period of instruction. While we would not wish to see all traditional teaching preserved for its own sake, it is nevertheless the case that it is in this setting, as well as in more contemporary approaches to learning and teaching, that we find a continuing need for assistance with such fundamental issues as using an overhead projector properly and preparing well-designed handouts.

We have addressed the challenge in three ways. First we have updated material from the previous edition on some of the more basic technologies, and retained a focus on materials and technologies rather than on approaches to teaching. Teaching approaches are covered elsewhere in this book, for example in the chapters on small groups and student-centred learning. Second, we have provided introductory ideas on using information technologies, and finally, we have distilled some principles of good practice that we believe apply to the use of all technologies and which provide a benchmark against which to evaluate what you are doing with your students.

BASIC PRINCIPLES IN PREPARING LEARNING AND TEACHING MATERIALS

In your teaching career, you will use quite a wide range of teaching materials and technologies. How you might produce and use them is the focus of this chapter. The fundamental criterion for judging the effectiveness of your teaching material is its audibility and/or visibility. If that seems too obvious to warrant mention, have a look at some of the materials used by others: overheads and slides with excessive amounts of tiny detail that cannot be read on the screen, complicated Web pages that look like art shows and take forever to download onto your computer, and faded handouts that cannot be read. Exaggeration? It does happen! When it does, it seriously interferes with the effectiveness of learning. Attention to the way in which the material is produced and how it is used in teaching will eliminate many of these problems.

Whether you are preparing a simple handout or multi-media materials, there are some basic principles that can be incorporated into your design and preparation which will enhance the quality and effectiveness of the material.

Relevance

Materials should be used in a way that is relevant to the purpose for which they were created and relevant to the students' level of understanding of the topic. Complex handouts distributed at the end of a lecture that are never referred to by the teacher are classic offenders of this principle.

Linkage

An introduction is usually required to establish the purpose of the material and to link it with what it is reasonable to expect students to know already.

Simplicity

Simplicity in the use of language and design, the avoidance of needless qualifications and the use of suitable abstractions of complex situations can be positive aids to understanding. For example, a simple line diagram may be more helpful in an explanation than a full-colour photograph or a complicated computer graphic.

Emphasis

Emphatic 'signs' can be incorporated into all teaching materials to stress important ideas, to indicate a change in the development of an argument, or to identify new material. Examples of emphasis include: headings and underlining in print, the use of colour and movement in Web pages, or statements such as 'this is a major factor' or 'to summarize these issues' on a sound recording or in a lecture.

Consistency in the use of pattern and style

Students acquire a 'feel' for the particular style you use to present material. Needless changing of style is only going to confuse them. In the increasingly corporatized world of modern education, many institutions have now adopted a house style. You should check for its application to the preparation of your teaching materials.

TYPES OF LEARNING AND TEACHING MATERIALS AND AIDS

With these basic principles in mind, the preparation and use of several basic types of teaching materials and aids will now be described. These are:

1.   the overhead projector;
2.   the 35 mm slide projector;

3. the video projector;
4. the whiteboard and blackboard;
5. video and film;
6. printed materials;
7. published material on the World Wide Web.

This list is by no means exhaustive. In keeping with the general thrust of this book, the intention is to get you started and to help you develop some confidence in the basic aspects of your teaching work.

1. The overhead projector

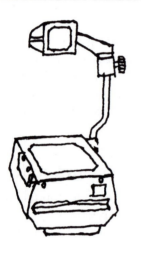

This valuable visual aid can project a wide range of transparency materials and silhouettes of opaque objects on to a screen positioned behind the lecturer. Because it can project both written and diagrammatic information, it reduces your need to engage in detailed descriptions and increases the opportunities for discussion with students. It also allows you to indicate material on the transparency without turning your back to the audience, an advantage over using a slide projector or a whiteboard.

The full benefit of the overhead projector will not be realized in your teaching unless you give careful attention to three things: the preparation of the transparency; the way the projector is set up in a room or lecture theatre; and the way you actually use it. We shall now turn to a consideration of each of these matters.

Transparency preparation

Figure 7.1 shows what a transparency looks like. In its basic form, it consists of an acetate sheet mounted on to a cardboard frame. Additional sheets of acetate on the same frame are known as 'overlays'. Overlays are particularly helpful to build up an idea as a presentation develops. Often, however, teachers dispense with the cardboard frame nowadays.

FIGURE 7.1 EXAMPLE OF TRANSPARENCY

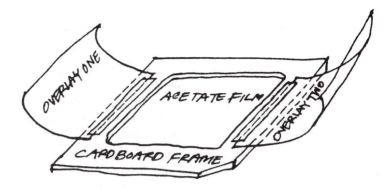

The following methods of making transparencies are available.

Felt pens: Felt pens containing water-soluble or permanent ink are available for making transparencies. Information is printed or drawn directly on to an acetate sheet. A suggested procedure is to place a piece of ruled paper underneath the acetate as a guide and write on the sheet. Another sheet of clean paper placed under your hand will prevent smudges from appearing on the acetate. Lettering should be no smaller than 5 mm in height, and preferably larger. Use black, blue, brown or green pens for lettering – avoid red, orange and yellow, which are difficult to read from a distance.

5MM LETTERS

Photocopying: Plain-paper photocopiers will accept acetate sheets, enabling the production of transparencies at the touch of a button. It is essential that the type of transparency sheet selected is suitable for use with the copier and that the original material is large and clear. Lettering, for example, must be at least 5 mm in height. Avoid the temptation to make overheads directly from books or from typed materials. In general, transparencies made in this way will be invisible to most of the class and therefore useless unless students are each given an exact copy of the transparency as a handout. If you wish to use such material, you should first make an enlargement.

Presentation packages: Software presentation packages (such as PowerPoint) give you a means of producing master sheets for high-quality transparencies. They also enable you to make and project transparencies electronically. If you are not already familiar with one of these packages, we recommend that you enrol in a short course to learn how to use it well. You will discover that making overheads is only the beginning! You will also be able to produce handouts, notes and multimedia presentations incorporating pictures, movies and sound as well as text and diagrams of many kinds. Your finished work can be presented as slides and overheads using video projectors or standard equipment, via the Internet, or through desktop computers. The time required to learn how to use a package will pay handsome dividends and open up a range of possibilities for you to make high-quality material.

When making overhead transparencies using this kind of software, remember the principle of simplicity – avoid the risk of overpowering your students with complex typefaces, distracting background designs and inappropriate colours. Learn some simple concepts of presentation design as well as how to master the technology.

Other uses of the overhead projector

There are other less orthodox ways in which you can use the overhead projector. Silhouettes of cardboard cut-outs or solid objects can be projected on to the screen. These may be coordinated with a prepared transparency. Transparent or translucent materials such as liquids in test tubes or biological specimens mounted on, or contained in, clear containers can also be prepared.

The guidelines listed in Figure 7.2 should be kept in mind when preparing an overhead transparency.

Setting up and using the overhead projector

In some situations, you will have flexibility when setting up the projector and screen. It is usual to place the

FIGURE 7.2   GUIDELINES
FOR MAKING AN EFFECTIVE
OVERHEAD TRANSPARENCY

Guidelines

- Limit each transparency to one main idea. Several simple transparencies are preferable to a complicated one.
- Reduce tabulated data to essential or to rounded figures. A single graph or diagram is often preferable.
- Lettering on overheads should be at least 5 mm, or at least 24 points in height, and preferably much larger. Titles and headings should be in the range 36–48 points.
- Learn to use one of the commercially available presentation packages as a tool for making overheads.

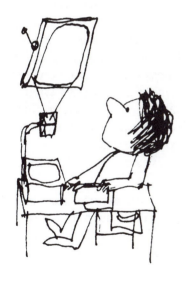

projector so that it is adjacent to the lectern or table from which you are working. Ensure that the projected image is square on the screen and free from angular and colour distortions. Angular distortions in the vertical axis can be overcome by tilting the top of the screen forward. Colour distortions, such as red or blue in the corners of the projected image, can usually be remedied by making an adjustment to the lamp. A control for this is often inside the projector. It is important to turn the electricity off at the plug before the adjustment is attempted.

Whenever a projector is moved, or before a presentation is commenced, the focus and position of the image must be checked. Once this is done, it is usually unnecessary to look at the screen again, particularly if you use a pen or pointer directly on the transparency. This enables you to maintain eye contact with students. If you wish to mask out part of the transparency, place a sheet of paper between the film and the glass stage of the projector. The weight of the transparency should prevent the paper from moving or falling away.

Remember to allow students plenty of time to read what you have projected. Many teachers find this difficult to do. One way is to read the transparency to yourself word for word. Also, make sure that anything you have to say complements the transparency. Do not expect students to listen to you and to look at something on the screen that is only vaguely related to what is being said. It is advisable to have the lamp on only when a transparency is being used in your teaching, otherwise the projected image or the large area of white light will distract the students' attention.

2. The 35 mm slide projector

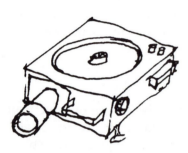

Much of what has been said about the overhead projector applies to slide projection. However, you will recognize that there are important differences between the two; one of these is that full-colour images can be used in slides. This may be an advantage, but with some material it could also be a disadvantage unless the students' level of understanding is sufficient to enable them to see what is relevant and pertinent in the material you are using. Slide interpretation can be aided by including in the photograph an appropriate reference point or a scale.

Slide preparation

The major error in slide-making is to assume that legibility in one medium, such as a table in a book or a journal, ensures slide legibility. Slides made from printed materials frequently contain too much detail and fine line work to enable them to be projected satisfactorily. This means that you may need to have artwork redrawn and new lettering added. Check any slides in your possession for legibility. A useful rule of thumb is that a slide that can be read without a magnifier is generally satisfactory. A better method is to go with a colleague to a large lecture theatre, project your slides and check to see if all the details are legible and understandable at the rear of the auditorium.

When making slides, avoid the temptation to put all the details on to the slide. If it is important for students to have all the details, provide these in a handout so that they can refer to it and keep it for reference. This ensures that they have accurate information on hand.

Photographers will advise you on the different processes available to produce your slides. These processes will usually include simple black-on-white slides, colour slides and diazo slides (white against blue, green or red backgrounds, the blue being preferred for clarity). Your institution may also be able to help you produce computer-generated colour slides of high quality. Another attractive way to prepare slides is to obtain negatives (white-on-black) and colour the white sections in by hand using coloured marking pens or translucent coloured paper designed for this purpose. The possibility exists of using separate colours to highlight different points on the slide. Whatever you choose, try to achieve a degree of consistency by sticking to one type of slide. Guidelines for the preparation of effective slides are given in Figure 7.3.

FIGURE 7.3 GUIDELINES FOR MAKING EFFECTIVE SLIDES

Guidelines

- Limit each slide to one main idea.
- Reduce tabulated data to essential or to rounded figures. Simple graphs and diagrams are to be preferred.
- When making new slides use a template with an aspect ratio of 3:2. An outline for typing of about 140 mm × 95 mm or 230 mm × 150 mm for artwork is suitable.

Setting up and using the slide projector

Slide-projection equipment is normally part of the standard fixtures in a lecture theatre, so the question of setting it up does not usually arise. If it does, locate the projector and screen with care to give the best view to students and so that it is convenient for you to operate the projector and room lights with a minimum of fuss. A remote-control device will be an invaluable aid.

Slide projection

Before loading your slides into a cartridge or carousel, carefully plan the sequence of their use. If your teaching is to be interspersed with slides, consider using black slides – this separates your material and means you don't have to keep turning the projector on and off or leave an inappropriate slide on view. Black slides are simply pieces of opaque film mounted in a slide frame to block off light to the screen and can easily be made from exposed film. If you plan to use the same slide on more than one occasion during a presentation, arrange to have duplicates made to save you and your students the agony of having to search back and forth through a slide series.

It is essential to have your slides marked or 'spotted' for projection (see Figure 7.4). As a check, the slides should be upside down with the emulsion side (ie the dull side) facing the screen. When showing your slides, it is rarely necessary to turn off all the lights. Remember that students may wish to take notes, so you should plan to leave some lights on or dim the main lights. Further advice on using slides is given in Chapter 5, on presenting a paper at a conference.

FIGURE 7.4 PROCEDURE FOR 'SPOTTING' SLIDES

Procedure

1. Place your slides on a light box (an overhead projector is ideal for this) so that the image is the same way up as it is to appear on the screen.
2. Turn the slide upside down.
3. Mark or number the slide in the top right-hand corner.

3. The video projector

This exciting device enables you to project a variety of materials from a computer on to a screen for large- and small-group viewing. These materials include videos, broadcast television, slides and overheads, multimedia presentations, computer output and Internet displays. When it is professionally set up, supported and used, the video projector is an outstanding presentation tool. Regrettably, this is not often the case, so you should approach the projector thoroughly well prepared and with back-up resources if you are not completely confident that things will work smoothly for you.

In our view, the current situation with video projectors must be approached with caution. The current technology is a good example of the embarrassing immaturity of much educational technology. If you doubt our judgement, have a close look at the systems currently in use with cords and cables everywhere, the need for back-up computers, incompatible software and systems, the risk of system crashes and so on.

Preparation

Your preparation involves four distinct matters: preparation of your material; preparation for your use of the equipment; preparation of the teaching room; and preparation of back-up resources.

The preparation of your material is covered elsewhere in this chapter; keep in mind the simple rule that, whatever material is used, it must be clearly visible and audible. We urge you to consider preparing back-up resources and alternative teaching strategies in case something goes wrong. For example, if you intend to be teaching in an unfamiliar environment, take overhead transparencies.

Equipment preparation can be broken down into understanding and preparing the computer hardware and software, the operation of the projector itself, and the way the projector and computer are linked together. These are matters that need to be addressed well before any use of equipment is undertaken before an audience. To believe you can sort matters out in front of an audience is to invite disaster. If you cannot get tuition or expert assistance, take time to study equipment manuals and try out the procedures well in advance of any teaching or presentation commitment.

As with all projection equipment, you will need to give consideration to the preparation of your video projector in relation to the room. In particular, review the position and focus of images on the screen, the level of illumination in the area of the screen, the position of equipment and the position from which you will be speaking in relation to the audience.

4. The whiteboard and blackboard

The whiteboard is a ubiquitous presentation tool found in many meeting rooms as well as in classrooms.

The principles of board use and preparation are outlined below. Do take care to use the correct pens with a whiteboard, as some can ruin its surface. Also, take care when cleaning a whiteboard. A dry cloth is often adequate, but sometimes you may need to use water, detergent or perhaps methylated spirits. Never use an abrasive cleaner, as it will scratch the surface and do irreparable damage to the board.

The colour of the pens you use is important. Black, dark blue and green are best. Avoid yellow, red and light colours, as these are difficult to read from a distance.

The blackboard (which may also be green) is still a commonly used visual aid and the one that you may use frequently, unless you rely exclusively on the overhead or video projector.

Few teachers give much thought to the material that they put on the board or to the way they use it. This is a pity. The results of the work are often ugly and indecipherable. Well-planned and well-used board work is a delight to see and is a valuable ally in presenting information accurately and clearly to your students.

Preparation

It is important to think ahead about your use of the board and make suitable comments in your teaching notes. Plan your use of the board by dividing the available space into a number of sections. Each section can then be used for a specific purpose such as references, diagrams, a summary of the structure of the lecture and so on.

Using a board

Some guidelines for using a board are given in Figure 7.5

FIGURE 7.5 GUIDELINES FOR USING BOARDS

Guidelines

- Start your teaching with a clean board. Clean your board when you have finished, both as a courtesy to the next class and also to reduce the likelihood of staining the board's surface.
- Try to avoid talking and writing on the board at the same time. When speaking, look at the students, not at the board.
- Face the board squarely and move across the board when writing. This will assist in writing horizontally.
- Stand aside when writing or drawing is completed to enable students to see the board.
- Concise information in skeleton note form is preferred to a 'newspaper' effect.
- Underline headings and important or unfamiliar words to give visual emphasis.
- Always give students a chance to copy down the information you have taken time to put on the board (if it is intended that they should have a copy).

- Use colours with discretion. Yellow and white are suitable colours for most written work on a blackboard, black and dark blue are best on white boards. Avoid using red, dark blue and green chalk as they are difficult to see and difficult to erase and avoid red and orange on white boards as they are relatively more difficult to read.

5. Video and film

Video gives you the opportunity to experiment with novel approaches when producing teaching materials, particularly now that relatively cheap cameras are available as well as presentation packages, both of which enable you to integrate video into a multimedia presentation. However, you should also become familiar with the range of suitable commercially available and Web-based materials before embarking on a career as a producer. You will find that several subject areas are well catered for in this regard.

Although the uses of video and film are similar, video does offer you several additional advantages, such as ease of production and relative cheapness. These factors have tended to make video a more popular medium than film.

Using video and film in teaching

As with many teaching aids, the uses of video and film are restricted only by your imagination and by the resources at your disposal. Some of the potential uses of video and film are described below:

- **As introductory material:** Video and film can be used at the start of a course of study to stimulate interest, to provide an overview or to form a basis for further learning and teaching. For example, a film on the effects of cigarette smoking could be used as an introduction for a study of lung cancer in health-education courses.

- **As a major source of information:** A constant flow of new ideas, techniques and procedures are a fact of life in most disciplines. Video and film can be used to disseminate this new information to your students or to professional meetings in which you may be involved. A further advantage of these media is that they can provide the viewer with vicarious experience which might be difficult or dangerous to obtain at first hand.

- **As a means of modelling:** This use is similar to the previous use, but you may find it helpful to produce material which demonstrates a technique or procedure in a clear step-by-step manner that students can watch and emulate at their own pace. An example might be a demonstration of how to conduct an appraisal interview in a management course.

- **As a stimulus for discussion:** Short, open-ended sections of video or film can be made to stimulate discussion among students. These are known as 'trigger films'. Students respond to the material as it is presented and both the stimulus and their responses to it are then discussed. We have found this process to be valuable for starting discussion about attitudes dealing with emotional situations. Sometimes, it is possible to locate suitable stimulus material in old films that would otherwise have no use.

- **As a means of distribution and relay:** Carefully placed video cameras can be used to send pictures to a separate viewing room, or even to relay them to remote locations. An obvious example of this is their use in operating theatres to enable a large number of medical students to witness an operation. Such an approach certainly provides advantages over traditional lecture theatre galleries.

- **As an information-storage system:** Video has a role to play in storing information for later teaching or for research use. For example, a recording can be made (with permission) of a particularly important event for subsequent review and analysis.

- **As a means of assembling visual and audio information:** In the past, video and film have been used to assemble a variety of information into one 'package'. Film clips, stills, models, interviews, recorded sounds and graphics could be recorded, assembled and edited to make a teaching programme. Today, presentation packages for your computer provide an accessible tool to achieve the same kind of outcome.

- **As a magnification medium:** Many teachers find that video is a handy tool to magnify the action or to display pictures of a demonstration. These can, of course, be recorded if needed for subsequent use.

The above list of video and film uses is by no means exhaustive, nor are the uses mutually exclusive in their application. For example, in teaching dentistry, video is used to magnify materials, to distribute and display these in a large laboratory (thus ensuring that all students are seeing the same thing), and sometimes to record the information as a resource for independent learning.

It is becoming less likely that you will be called on to produce videos for use in teaching. However, if you are, we recommend that you review the guidelines on making educational videos contained in earlier editions of this book.

6. Printed material

Books, journals, handouts and study guides carry a very large part of the instructional burden in teaching, and will continue to do so. Yet often, surprisingly little thought is given by university teachers to the design and use of these important teaching materials.

Design

We strongly recommend Hartley's book as a reference to have beside you. Care needs to be taken in designing and

preparing printed materials. Over-organization of the text does not help the reader and may actually interfere with learning. You will find it helpful to standardize layouts. For example, in a paper-based system, you may wish to institute a system of different coloured papers for the different kinds of material you prepare for students (eg white for lecture notes, green for bibliographies, yellow for exercises). The basic principles for layout and design of printed materials are outlined in Figure 7.6.

The variety of fonts available in personal-computer software makes it necessary to select with care. Have a look at the typographical layouts in better-quality newspapers and journals for ideas that you can put into practice.

Using printed material

Handouts can serve a number of useful purposes in your teaching, but this medium is frequently misused because the material is often simply distributed to students, then quickly forgotten. Remember that you can produce handouts with presentation software to support a formal lecture and that you can distribute them via the Internet.

Handouts can be used by students as a note-taking guide to a lecture. Supplementary information, or perhaps a copy of a paper that you think is important, can also be given in a handout.

How you use the handout in your teaching is a crucial matter. We suggest that you direct students' attention to the handout by discussing a particular definition, reading through a brief list of points with students or asking them to fill in some part of it with additional information. If your students have to use the handout in the teaching session, it is likely that they will remember it and not simply file it away to be forgotten.

FIGURE 7.6 GUIDELINES FOR DESIGN OF PRINTED MATERIALS

Guidelines

Incorporating the following can enhance learning from printed materials:

- An introduction to relate the new material to the past experience of the student.
- A summary of the major ideas or arguments presented.
- The use of major and minor headings.
- Space between paragraphs and sections to relieve the impact of too much print.
- Simplicity in expression.
- Appropriately labelled illustrations, tables and graphs (a series of diagrams building up to a complete concept may be more helpful than one detailed diagram).
- Questions and exercises within the text to stimulate thinking.

Prescribed reading

Prescribed reading of textbooks and journals is another matter that warrants your careful attention. Some teachers swamp their students with lists of books and articles to be read and give little thought to how students might manage the task. If you want the students to undertake some reading, then consider the following points:

- What are students expected to achieve by undertaking the reading? Make this purpose clearly known to the students.
- How will the reading be followed up in subsequent teaching?
- Will the recommended reading be readily available in libraries, through bookshops or on the Web?

● How can the reading be usefully organized? Arrange the material in a logical fashion, indicate why an item has been listed and what is especially important about it.

7. **Publishing material on the World Wide Web**

Preparing and publishing your own material on the Web should not be too difficult a task, particularly if you can enlist the assistance of locally available expertise to get you through the main technical issues. If you cannot locate such direct assistance, then we suggest that you either visit your local bookshop or computer retailer for the most recent books and software on the topic or seek online help on a current Web site.

As the 'Internet revolution' matures, the tools you need are becoming simpler. At the time of writing, the following general directions were valid. All you will need is a computer with a connection to the Internet and a 'Web browser', which is the software that allows you to navigate through the different sites on the Web.

The basic steps are:

1. Prepare your material. Your word processor may have an automatic 'Save as... HTML' option under the File menu. If you save your work in this format, it will be ready for placement on the Web. This is the easiest option for preparing your material. The drawbacks are that some formatting may be lost and some punctuation marks altered. You also miss out on using more versatile Web-building tools that can offer greater options (images, page colour, links to other sites etc). This means that the way you wish to present your material may be affected.

2. Another option for preparing your work for the Web is to access free online Web-page builders, available from sites such as Geocities (www.geocities.com) or

The Globe (www.theglobe.com). Alternatively, you can purchase one of the several entry-level Web-page design software packages such as Adobe Pagemill or Netscape Composer. These packages come with helpful paper-based guides and they will enable you to save your work in a format that is ready for publication on the Web.

3. Once your material is ready for the Web you need to place it on a 'server'. This is a computer dedicated to the task of allowing viewers to access your page from anywhere at any time. For teaching uses, server space will usually be available from your institution. Space is also available through ISPs (Internet Service Providers). Alternatively, you may wish to take advantage of free server space offered by many sites on the Web – you will pay a price, however, usually in the form of a banner advertisement that pops up when someone views your page!

Once you have mastered the above steps, you're done! Details on all the points above are available on the Web itself. If you are using or plan to use Netscape Composer, Netscape provides an excellent step-by-step guide (http://home.mcom.com/browsers/createsites/index.html).

As with all teaching preparation, you need a clear idea of what you are trying to achieve and for whom you are preparing the material. Assuming that the material is for your students, you could provide them with a diversity of resources to assist them with their learning, such as links to helpful learning resources, assignments and general feedback, reading material, examples of exemplary student work and so on. Alternatively, you may be planning to teach interactively via the World Wide Web. In both of these cases, we urge you to review the currently available literature on the topic, some of which is identified in the guided reading section.

USING TECHNOLOGY IN LEARNING AND TEACHING

New technologies are having a significant impact on learning and teaching in higher education, and will continue to do so. As we have already seen in this chapter and elsewhere in the book, computer and communication technologies can enhance a wide range of traditional teaching activities from the production and distribution of materials to the ways in which learners and teachers interact with each other. But these are examples of the ways in which technology replicates traditional teaching.

It is now clear that the forces of change are combining to move us to different ways of learning and teaching in which we will see more of the following developments:

● students becoming more active and independent in their learning;
● students working collaboratively with each other rather than competitively;
● teachers becoming more like designers and managers of learning resources, and guides for their students rather than dispensers and controllers of information;
● rapidly changing curriculum content reflecting freedom to access a diverse range of ever-expanding resources for learning;
● more effective assessment with a growing emphasis on assessment for learning.

How can you respond to these new and challenging demands, and where can you learn more? Of course, we hope that the material in this book will assist you with the basics of learning, teaching and assessment issues. But how can you learn more about the technologies (if these are new to you), and how can you keep abreast of developments? These matters are well beyond the scope of this book, but we hope the following will be helpful.

GUIDED READING

For those new to technology, and in particular the technologies applied in higher education, we recommend two complementary books. The first is by Warren, Brunner, Maier and Barnett, and is called *Technology in Teaching and Learning, An introductory guide*. The second is by the same authors and is called *Using Technology in Teaching and Learning*. Both were published by Kogan Page in 1998. The first book is ideal for the beginner and takes the reader in clear steps through fundamental technical matters arranged as follows: getting material into and out of your computer; how to get connected to the Internet; using Internet resources; communicating using computers; and using the World Wide Web. The second book builds upon the fundamentals, and explores ways in which computers can be used to support the teaching of large groups, to deliver learning resources to students, and for communication between students.

If you want to go further and explore some of the ways in which you can use the Internet in your teaching, we suggest Ian Forsyth's *Teaching and Learning Materials and the Internet* (Second Edition, Kogan Page, 1998).

To maintain your currency in the uses of technology beyond the material in these books, we urge you to monitor literature in books, journals and particularly in the electronic resources of the kind available on the World Wide Web.

There is a rapidly growing number of books as well as resources on the World Wide Web that can assist you with some of the educational issues of using technology in education. We suggest the following three books:

Brooks, David W (1997) *Web Teaching*, Plenum Press, New York and London.

Inglis, Alastair, Ling, Peter and Joosten, Vera (1999) *Delivering Digitally: Managing the transition to the knowledge media*, Kogan Page, London.

Phillips, Rob (1997) *The Developer's Handbook to Interactive Multimedia: A practical guide for educational applications*, Kogan Page, London.

If you are concerned with evaluating materials and educational technologies, we suggest Martin Tessmer's *Planning and Conducting Formative Evaluations* (Kogan Page, London, 1993). This is an interesting mixture of useful guidance on planning evaluation, the evaluation of materials and the whole notion of formative evaluation. Hartley's book (see below) is also helpful on evaluating materials.

Books referred to in this chapter

The Third Edition of *Designing Instructional Text* by J Hartley (Kogan Page, London, 1994) is highly recommended for preparing text-based materials (books, manuals, handouts, computer-generated or stored text). We used Hartley when preparing this book.

You will note that our publisher, Kogan Page, produces a good range of up-to-date sources. To help you keep in contact with developments, we suggest you browse their Web site (www.kogan-page.co.uk).

And a final thought...

Learning is ultimately a human activity, regardless of the technology used.

Herb Simon, quoted in W J McKeachie, 'Student ratings, the validity of use', *American Psychologist*, November, 1997, p. 1224.

Chapter 8   Curriculum Planning

INTRODUCTION

This chapter aims to assist you when you become
involved in some way in curriculum planning and wish to
do so in a systematic manner. Unfortunately, there is no
straightforward formula to guide you in this activity. The
reasons for this are as follows. First, curriculum planning
is a complex business involving more than purely educational considerations. For example, you will find that full
account must be taken of the political and economic
context in which you teach. Second, relatively few courses
are started from scratch. Much curriculum development
is a matter of revising and adapting existing courses or
materials. And third, there are important differences
between individuals – especially between individuals
working in different disciplines – in the ways in which
they view a variety of educational issues. You may, for
instance, see your main function as transmitting appropriate knowledge, skills and attitudes. On the other hand
you may perceive your role as being primarily concerned
with the personal and social development of your
students as well as with their intellectual development.
In a book of this kind it is not possible to provide a
discussion which can fully take into account these various
orientations. However, we believe that you should be
aware of these differences and we would encourage you to
read further on the matter to help develop your own
particular orientation and your own approach to
curriculum development. Our reference to Biggs and to
Toohey at the end of this chapter is a useful starting point
for your reading.

In our view, the key to curriculum planning is to forge
educationally sound and logical links between planned

intentions (expressed as objectives), course content, teaching and learning methods, and the assessment of student learning while taking account of student characteristics. In the past, too many courses started with vague intentions, and consisted of teaching which had a tenuous relationship to these intentions and employed methods of assessment which bore little or no relationship to either. Such courses then placed students in the unfortunate situation of playing a guessing game, with their academic future as the stake! This pattern can be improved by adopting an approach which links the intentions with course content, teaching, and the assessment. The approach is now called 'alignment', and is achieved when the objectives express the kind of understanding we expect from students, the teaching encourages and supports students to undertake activities likely to achieve those understandings, and the assessment tasks tell students what is required and also show whether the objectives have been met. We urge you to look at the book by Biggs, in which this important idea is more fully developed. These elements of curriculum planning, together with a consideration of students, are the focus of this chapter.

Curriculum development should be an ongoing process. In practice, curriculum development can and does start with any of the linked elements named above and we have no desire to alter that practice. Indeed, our major concern is to ensure that each element – intentions, teaching and learning, assessment, content – **is** considered and that the links between the elements are thoughtfully made.

WHO SHOULD BE RESPONSIBLE FOR CURRICULUM PLANNING?

Although we assume you have some responsibility for curriculum planning it is unlikely that this will be a solo

affair. You will have additional resources on which to draw which may include staff in your own and related departments, staff of a university teaching unit, members of your discipline outside your immediate environment and students. These people may form a planning committee or a panel of advisers. Whatever your situation, experience suggests that some form of consultation with others is very desirable.

COURSE CONTENT

Content is a broad concept meant to include all aspects of knowledge, skills and attitudes relevant to the course **and** to the intellectual experiences of students and their teachers in a course.

While not always easy to achieve, we feel that course content should be made explicit and that this will then put you in a better position to make informed and coherent decisions in your curriculum planning. There are several different criteria for selecting content that may be more or less relevant to your work. These criteria are presented below for your consideration.

Philosophical criteria

These criteria focus attention on theoretical, methodological and value positions. For example:

- Content should be a means of enhancing the intellectual development of students, not an end in itself.
- Content that is solely concerned with technical matters has no place in a university education; content must also involve moral and ethical considerations.
- Content should help contribute to a deep rather than to a surface view of knowledge.

Professional criteria

These criteria recognize that courses in the professions may reflect explicit legal and professional requirements before practice is permitted:

- Content must provide the kinds of theoretical and practical experiences required for registration.
- Content should include attention to professional ethics.

Psychological criteria

These criteria relate to the application of psychological principles – especially of learning theory – to teaching:

- Content should be carefully integrated to avoid fragmentation and consequential loss of opportunities for students to develop 'deep' approaches to learning (see Chapter 1).
- Content selection must provide opportunities to emphasize and to develop higher-level intellectual skills such as reasoning, problem-solving, critical thinking and creativity.
- Content should provide opportunities for the development of attitudes and values.
- Content should be selected to assist in the development of students as independent lifelong learners.

Practical criteria

These criteria concern the feasibility of teaching something and may relate to resource considerations:

- Content may be derived from one or two major texts because of a lack of suitable alternative materials.
- Content should be influenced by the availability of a 'key' teaching resource: library materials, information-technology resources, people, patients, physical environment, etc.

Student criteria

These criteria relate to the characteristics of the students you teach. We consider these criteria to be so important in curriculum planning that a full section is devoted to them. Student criteria may affect the choice of content (and ways of teaching and assessing) in a variety of ways:

- Content may be selected to reflect the background, needs and interests of all students.
- Content should be matched to the intellectual and maturity level of students.
- Content might take account of the diverse life experiences of students.

How you actually go about selecting content will largely be determined by the kind of person you are (especially by your views regarding the relative importance of your role as a teacher, the role of students and course content), the norms and practices in the discipline you teach and, increasingly, the demands of the educational market.

STUDENTS

Taking account of student characteristics, needs and interests is the most difficult part of curriculum planning. The reason for this is that teachers now face increasingly heterogenous groups of students and, at the same time, must take account of legislative requirements to address specific issues such as occupational health and equal opportunities. It is no longer enough to state that curriculum planners needs to 'take account of students' and then to proceed as if they did not exist. This process must be quite formal and perhaps even negotiated between a staff member and students. For instance, in most graduate programmes, and in some humanities and social science undergraduate courses, topics and assessment arrangements are decided in a consultative fashion.

On the other hand, student influence may be less explicit but nevertheless very powerful, especially, for example, in professional courses where students may convey their impatience with basic science or theoretical coursework that are perceived as irrelevant yet are a prerequisite for subsequent study.

'Taking account' of students is partly your responsibility and partly your institution's responsibility. Institutional responsibilities – which we would encourage you to influence positively – might include:

- the provision of special physical facilities to assist students with a disability in courses;
- tutorial assistance in the English language, especially for non-native speakers and international students;
- bridging courses and foundation courses to assist in the process of adjustment to higher education.

Your responsibilities are no less onerous. In addition to accommodating the wide range of personalities, learning styles, social backgrounds, expectations and academic achievement of direct-entry students from school, you must also be prepared to teach students from other backgrounds and with 'different' characteristics than your own. Six examples of current concern which we will briefly discuss are: women, mature-age students, students with a disability, first-year students, indigenous students and international students.

Women students

The role of women and women students in higher education has received a lot of attention. In curriculum planning you should consider:

- The selection of suitable course content that at least acknowledges that women comprise half the human race: thus, for example, the selection of women writers in English feminist perspectives in history, and the work of women in science and technology are matters for attention.

● The elimination of sexist language in course materials and in teaching.

You will be aware that many governments now view these issues as so important that there are legal sanctions for transgressions. As your institution is likely to have formal policies relating to equal opportunities, you should seek out this information and relate it to your curriculum planning.

Adult (mature-age) students

This group brings a rich diversity of experiences. Older students usually approach higher education with a greater intensity of purpose than their younger peers because so much more, in terms of sacrifices and ambitions, rests on their study and achievements. They also expect staff to be more flexible and adaptive in their teaching and assessment methods. These students often experience greater anxiety over assessment arrangements. Vagueness on your part, or in the course plan, can only contribute to this concern.

Students with a disability

You will encounter students whose hearing or sight are mildly or severely impaired, who have medical disabilities, psychiatric or psychological disabilities, or who have a learning disability. Most universities have policies and support arrangements relating to students who have disabilities of these kinds, and we urge you to understand the resources that are available to help you when teaching and assessing students with a disability.

First-year students

The teaching of this group is of particular concern because of their need to adjust to the learning environment of higher education. Some students will belong to a group with specific needs (eg mature-age or international students). The sensitive use of small group work (see Chapter 3) can be a means of dealing with some matters, but not all. The selection of content – taking care to induct students into the language and peculiarities of your subject and to the assessment methods – and above all, the clarity of your expectations, can all contribute to a smooth and successful transition.

Indigenous students

Indigenous students, especially those in their first year of studies, may require special consideration. These considerations relate most closely to matters of your personal preparation for teaching. Two important aspects of preparation are your own level of cultural awareness and the way in which you teach. Cultural awareness can be developed through training programmes, but a more realistic approach for the busy teacher is to develop out-of-class contact with relevant support groups and through reading.

International students

The usual principles of good teaching apply as much for this group as for others but particular care should be given to your use of language – especially your speed, pronunciation and use of unnecessarily complex sentence constructions. You may need to direct them to support services that are sure to exist in your institution.

As you review these considerations for each group of students you will realize that almost all are worthwhile principles for planning and teaching **all** students and should therefore be taken into account in routine curriculum planning. In summary, we offer the following general suggestion: Be aware of your own attitudes and behaviour, be available and helpful to **all** students and, particularly, be willing to learn, to adapt and to adjust. A tall order, we know. But elsewhere in this book you will find suggestions on ways of developing these qualities. Of particular relevance is Chapter 1 on student learning.

As we remarked in our introduction, there is no straight-forward formula to guide you in curriculum planning. Nowhere is this more evident than in the process of linking the many content and student considerations we have been discussing to the particulars of preparing a course plan. We suggest that you prepare a simple check-list of content and student matters to be taken into account during the next step of curriculum planning – writing course objectives.

AIMS AND OBJECTIVES

The intentions of the course are usually expressed in the form of aims and objectives. Aims are general statements of intent. Objectives are rather more specific statements of what students should be able to do as a result of a course of study. We are convinced that clear objectives are a fundamental tool in curriculum planning because they enable the rational choice of content and teaching and learning activities and are important in planning a valid assessment. Objectives provide a guide to teachers and to students, but should not be so restrictive as to prevent the spontaneity that is so essential to the higher education of students. The relationship between objectives, teaching and learning activities, and assessment is best set out in a course planning chart (see Figure 8.1).

Each defined objective is matched with appropriate teaching and learning activities and with a valid form of assessment. For instance, in the example, you would not expect the students to learn to be able to 'take a comprehensive history at the completion of the course' on the basis of lectures, nor would you expect that this could be validly assessed by a paper-and-pencil test. The course designer has provided a relevant teaching and learning activity and a suitable form of assessment.

FIGURE 8.1 EXAMPLE OF A
COURSE PLANNING CHART

OBJECTIVES	TEACHING AND LEARNING ACTIVITIES	ASSESSMENTS
AT THE COMPLETION OF THE COURSE THE STUDENT WILL BE ABLE TO: **1** TAKE A COMPREHENSIVE HISTORY	**1** PRECEPTOR SESSIONS WITH REVIEW OF VIDEO RECORDINGS OF PATIENT INTERVIEWS	**1** PRECEPTOR'S JUDGEMENT BASED ON VIDEO RECORDING OF A HISTORY AT THE END OF COURSE
2 **3**	**2** **3**	**2** **3**

WRITING OBJECTIVES

Before you start writing objectives it might help to know what they look like. Here are some examples:

- Know the basic terminology of the subject (a general objective).
- Understand the changing relationship between money income and real income as prices change (Economics).
- Derive pressure drop and heat-transfer relations for flow in smooth pipes (Engineering).
- Obtain a problem-orientated history from a patient (Medicine).
- Develop a scholarly concern for accuracy (general attitudinal objective).
- Defend one's judgements against the informed criticism of peers (English).

In each case, the objective contains a statement which suggests the kind of behaviour that students will be required to demonstrate in order to show that the objective has been achieved. Now, if you look at each objective again, you will notice that they suggest rather different kinds of behaviour. The first three objectives require information of an intellectual kind for their achievement and may be classified as **knowledge objectives**. The fourth objective refers to a skill of a practical kind and is thus described as a **skill objective**. The fifth objective suggest an attitude of mind and is therefore classified as an **attitudinal objective**. The last objective demands a knowledge background, as well as the skills of intellectual debate and argument.

The three broad divisions – knowledge, skills and attitudes – are often used in grouping objectives but you may come across several refinements of each division in the literature. The most common of these refinements is the taxonomy developed by Bloom and his colleagues. They call the three divisions 'domains': cognitive (knowledge and intellectual skills), psychomotor (physical skills) and affective (feelings and attitudes). These domains have been further subdivided to provide hierarchies of objectives of increasing complexity.

Knowledge objectives (the cognitive domain): It is in this area that Bloom's taxonomy has been most widely applied. He proposes six levels:

- knowledge;
- comprehension;
- application;
- analysis;
- synthesis; and
- evaluation.

The reason for keeping different levels in mind when writing objectives is that courses sometimes pay undue attention to one level (usually the recall of information).

Skill objectives (the psychomotor domain): Bloom and his colleagues did not develop a hierarchy of objectives in the psychomotor domain, though others have attempted to do so. In many courses, teachers need to pay a great deal of attention to developing skill objectives. Such objectives may be improved if the condition under which the performance is to occur, and the criteria of acceptable performance, can be indicated.

One way you might find useful is to specify competent performance using the hierarchy developed by Korst. He suggests that there will be some skills with which one would expect students to show a high degree of competence and others with which one might only expect familiarity. His hierarchy is: well-qualified or very competent; familiar with or competent; awareness or minimal familiarity.

Attitudinal objectives (the affective domain): Writing objectives in the affective area is very difficult, which possibly explains why they are so often ignored. This is unfortunate because, implicity or explicitly, there are many attitudinal qualities we hope to see in our graduating students. As Krathwohl has a taxonomy in this domain you could approach the task in much the same way as writing knowledge objectives.

Another way is to attempt to define the starting attitudes of the students and match these with more desirable attitudes towards which you would hope they would move. For example, you could be concerned with the attitude of students to something. You might start by assuming that the students had a stereotyped attitude. You would then wish to move them away from this towards an attitude which demonstrated understanding and acceptance of other views. The advantage of this method is that it recognizes that not all students will develop the desired attitude nor will they all necessarily start a course with the same attitudes. The way to express objectives using this approach is to state 'Away from... (a particular attitude), towards... (a desirable attitude)'.

Where do objectives come from?

Writing objectives is not simply a process of sitting, pen in hand, waiting for inspiration, although original thinking is certainly encouraged. Objectives will come from a careful consideration of the subject matter, what you and your colleagues know about students and about the subject. This will not be an easy task. You should consider a wide range of sources for objectives. These include:

- an analysis of your own and colleagues' knowledge, skills and attitudes;
- ways of thinking and problem-solving to be developed;
- students' interests, needs and characteristics;
- subject matter, as reflected in the published literature (especially in suitable textbooks);
- the needs of society;
- the requirements of professional certifying authorities or commercial clients for educational services;
- the objectives of the department or faculty.

How specific and detailed should objectives be?

This is a question frequently asked. The answer depends on the purposes for which the objectives are to be used. In designing a course, the objectives will be more general than the objectives for a particular teaching session within the course. As objective writing can become tedious, trivial and time-consuming it is best to keep your objectives simple, unambiguous and broad enough to convey clearly your intentions. To illustrate from our own field of teaching, the objectives for a six-week clinical skills course, conducted for groups of 9–10 fifth-year students, are shown below. Though quite broad, these objectives have proved detailed enough for course planning purposes and for making the intentions of the programme clear to students.

FIGURE 8.2   EXAMPLE OF
COURSE OBJECTIVES

OBJECTIVES	TEACHING AND LEARNING ACTIVITIES	ASSESSMENTS
AT THE COMPLETION OF THE COURSE THE STUDENT WILL BE ABLE TO		
1 TAKE A COMPREHENSIVE HISTORY	**1**	**1**
2 PERFORM A COMPLETE PHYSICAL EXAMINATION	**2**	**2**
3 WRITE UP THE HISTORY AND EXAMINATION AND CONSTRUCT A PROBLEM LIST	**3**	**3**
4 MAKE DECISIONS ON DIAGNOSIS, INVESTIGATION AND MANAGEMENT	**4**	**4**
5 RELATE WELL TO PATIENTS	**5**	**5**
6 SHOW THAT HE/SHE HAS IMPROVED HIS/HER KNOWLEDGE OF MEDICINE AND SURGERY	**6**	**6**

CHOOSING METHODS AND RELATING OBJECTIVES TO TEACHING AND LEARNING ACTIVITIES

The methods you employ to achieve the objectives should not only allow those objectives to be realized, but will also reflect the kind of orientation you have to curriculum planning. If your orientation is primarily the transmission of content, it is likely that your teaching methods will be dominated by lectures, assigned reading of books and electronically based materials and set problem-solving exercises; if it is to the intellectual and personal development of your students, small group teaching or individual tutorials and e-mail discussions are likely to play a more important role.

The actual choice of methods will be governed by several factors. Among the most important will be:

- ensuring that students engage in appropriate learning activities;
- your own expertise in using different methods;
- technical and financial resources to support the method you wish to use.

Before leaving this subject we should like you to consider one important matter about choice of methods. Courses are often constructed in ways that reveal a growing complexity of subject matter. For example, early in the first year there may be an emphasis on basic principles and ideas. In later years, subject matter may be very much more complex and demanding. Yet, in our experience, the teaching methods used in the later years to not generally demand higher levels of intellectual performance and personal involvement.

The main types of teaching in higher education, such as lecturing, small group teaching and practical teaching, are dealt with in earlier chapters. These are by no means all of the methods available. Other possibilities include field-work, peer teaching and a variety of technology-based techniques. In addition, it should be remembered that students undertake many learning activities in the absence of teaching and there is growing pressure for this to become more common. It is reasonable to make explicit in your objectives areas where you expect the students to work on their own. This particularly applies to knowledge objectives which might be achieved just as well independently in a library or by accessing the Web. It could also apply to some skill objectives where students might be expected to seek out relevant experience by themselves.

FIGURE 8.3 EXAMPLE OF MATCHING TEACHING AND LEARNING ACTIVITIES TO COURSE OBJECTIVES

OBJECTIVES	TEACHING AND LEARNING ACTIVITIES	ASSESSMENTS
AT THE COMPLETION OF THE COURSE THE STUDENT WILL BE ABLE TO **1** TAKE A COMPREHENSIVE HISTORY	**1** PRECEPTOR SESSIONS WITH REVIEW OF VIDEO RECORDINGS OF PATIENT INTERVIEWS.	
2 PERFORM A COMPLETE PHYSICAL EXAMINATION	**2** VIEWING DEMONSTRATION VIDEOTAPE. PRECEPTOR SESSIONS WITH PATIENTS. WARD PRACTICE. WARD ROUNDS WITH RESIDENT STAFF.	
3 WRITE UP THE HISTORY AND EXAMINATION AND CONSTRUCT PROBLEM LIST	**3** HANDOUT OF EXEMPLAR CASE HISTORY. WRITE-UPS ON WARD PATIENTS. PRECEPTOR SESSIONS TO CHECK AND DISCUSS WRITE-UPS.	
4 MAKE DECISIONS ON DIAGNOSIS, INVESTIGATIONS AND MANAGEMENT	**4** PROBLEM-BASED WHOLE GROUP DISCUSSION SESSIONS. REVIEW OF CASE WRITE-UPS.	
5 RELATE WELL TO PATIENTS	**5** PRECEPTOR SESSIONS WITH REVIEW OF VIDEO RECORDINGS OF PATIENT INTERVIEWS.	
6 SHOW THAT HE/SHE HAS IMPROVED HIS/HER KNOWLEDGE OF MEDICINE AND SURGERY	**6** INDEPENDENT LEARNING. PREPARATION OF CASES FOR PRESENTATION. TAPE-SLIDE TUTORIALS. COMPUTERIZED SELF-ASSESSMENT PROGRAMMES.	

The way in which this process has been followed through in the clinical skills course we have already introduced is demonstrated once again on the course planning chart (Figure 8.3). When planning this course we were aware that many students needed assistance with their basic history-taking and physical examination skills. We thus decided to put the majority of our staff time into achieving the first two objectives. The most appropriate teaching method was obviously direct observation with feedback and as this is very time-consuming we opted for a preceptor system where one staff member was responsible for only three students throughout the programme. However, opportunity was also provided for students to obtain additional ward practice on their own and the resident staff were also mobilized to provide further help and instruction in this area. One of the implications of this decision on staff allocation was to accept that the sixth objective (improving their knowledge in the subjects Medicine and Surgery) would have to be achieved by other methods. This has involved an expectation that students accept responsibility for doing much of this themselves. We have also designed and prepared a variety of self-instructional materials. Other teaching techniques are incorporated to achieve other objectives.

RELATING OBJECTIVES TO ASSESSMENT METHODS

Just as it is important to match the teaching and learning activities methods with the objectives, it is important to match the assessment methods to the objectives. Failure to do so is an important reason why courses fail to live up to expectations. A mismatch of assessment and objectives may lead to serious distortions of student learning because, whether we like it or not, the assessment plans and activities tell students what we want them to learn.

In designing your course, we believe that it is important to distinguish carefully between two types of assessment. One is primarily designed to give feedback to the students as they go along (**formative assessment**). The other is to assess their abilities for the purposes of grading (**summative assessment**). Formative assessment is a crucial part of the educational process, especially where complex intellectual and practical skills are to be mastered. Such assessment is notoriously deficient in many courses in higher education.

The way in which assessment was designed in the example of our clinical skills course is shown in Figure 8.4. As no formal examination is required at the completion of the course, the major emphasis of the assessment activities is formative. However, assessment activities of a summative type are conducted during the final two weeks of the programme when aspects of the student's performance are observed by preceptors and by other staff members. You will note that the assessment of knowledge is left largely to the students themselves. In other circumstances we might have used a written test to assess this component of the course.

SEQUENCING AND ORGANIZING THE COURSE

It is unlikely that the way in which you have set out your objectives, teaching and assessment on the planning chart will be the best chronological or practical way to present the course to students. There are several things that must be done. Firstly, there must be a **grouping** of related objectives and activities. (In the example we are following throughout this chapter, such a grouping occurs for objectives one to three which are largely to be achieved by the preceptor sessions.) Secondly, there must be a **sequencing** of the teaching activities. There are likely to be circumstances in your own context that influence you to sequence a course in a particular way, such as semesters or teaching terms. However, there are also a number

FIGURE 8.4 EXAMPLE OF MATCHING
ASSESSMENT PROCEDURES TO
COURSE OBJECTIVES

OBJECTIVES	TEACHING AND LEARNING ACTIVITIES	ASSESSMENTS
AT THE COMPLETION OF THE COURSE THE STUDENT WILL BE ABLE TO		
1 TAKE A COMPREHENSIVE HISTORY	**1** PRECEPTOR SESSIONS WITH REVIEW OF VIDEO RECORDINGS OF PATIENT INTERVIEWS.	**1** ASSESSMENT OF VIDEO RECORDING DURING COURSE (FORMATIVE). ASSESSMENT OF VIDEO RECORDING AT END OF COURSE (SUMMATIVE).
2 PERFORM A COMPLETE PHYSICAL EXAMINATION	**2** VIEWING DEMONSTRATION VIDEO TAPE. PRECEPTOR SESSIONS WITH PATIENTS. WARD PRACTICE. WARD ROUNDS WITH RESIDENT STAFF.	**2** DIRECT OBSERVATION DURING COURSE (FORMATIVE). DIRECT OBSERVATION AT END OF COURSE (SUMMATIVE).
3 WRITE UP THE HISTORY AND EXAMINATION AND CONSTRUCT A PROBLEM LIST	**3** HANDOUT OF EXEMPLAR CASE HISTORY. WRITE-UPS ON WARD PATIENTS. PRECEPTOR SESSIONS TO CHECK AND DISCUSS WRITE-UPS.	**3** MARKING AND DISCUSSION OF CASE WRITE-UPS DURING COURSE (FORMATIVE). MARKING OF CASE WRITE-UPS AT END OF COURSE (SUMMATIVE).
4 MAKE DECISIONS ON DIAGNOSIS INVESTIGATION AND MANAGEMENT	**4** PROBLEM-BASED WHOLE GROUP DISCUSSION SESSIONS. REVIEW OF CASE WRITE-UPS.	**4** PERFORMANCE IN WHOLE GROUP SESSIONS (SUMMATIVE).
5 RELATE WELL TO PATIENTS	**5** PRECEPTOR SESSIONS WITH REVIEW OF VIDEO-RECORDINGS OF PATIENT INTERVIEWS.	**5** ASSESSMENT OF VIDEO RECORDINGS DURING COURSE (FORMATIVE AND SUMMATIVE).
6 SHOW THAT HE/SHE HAS IMPROVED HIS/HER KNOWLEDGE OF MEDICINE AND SURGERY	**6** INDEPENDENT LEARNING. PREPARATION OF CASES FOR PRESENTATION. COMPUTERISED SELF-ASSESSMENT PROGRAMMES.	**6** SELF-ASSESSMENT. COMPUTERIZED SELF-ASSESSMENT PROGRAMMES (FORMATIVE).

of educational grounds upon which to base the sequencing. These include:

- proceeding from what students know to what they do not know;
- proceeding from concrete experiences to abstract reasoning;
- the logical or historical development of a subject;
- important themes or concepts;
- starting from unusual, novel or complex situations and working backwards towards understanding.

As our understanding of how different factors can influence learning advances, you should give consideration to the ways in which you can facilitate deep-learning approaches by your students through the way in which you organize and manage the course and the kinds of intellectual and assessment demands you place on students. We suggest that you review the relevant sections in Chapter 1 on helping students learn to guide you in your consideration of this important matter.

Finally, you will need to consider the broad organizing principles behind your course. Will you, for example, offer it in a traditional way with a set timetable of carefully sequenced learning activities culminating in an end-of-year examination? Will you design your course around a completely different approach such as problem-based learning, or will you make the learning opportunities for your students more flexible? If you propose to move to a different approach, and we would generally encourage this based on our understanding of effective learning, we suggest you look at Chapter 2 on student-centred learning.

OTHER COURSE DESIGN CONSIDERATIONS

Many of the important educational considerations in designing a course have been addressed, but there are other matters that must be dealt with before a course can be mounted. These are only briefly described because the way in which they are handled depends very much on the administrative arrangements of the particular situation in which you teach. Having said that, we are not suggesting in any way that your educational plans must be subservient to administrative considerations. Clearly, in the best of all possible worlds, the administrative considerations would be entirely subservient to the educational plans but the reality is that there will be a series of trade-offs, with educational considerations hopefully paramount.

In planning your new course, you will need to take the following into account.

Administrative responsibilities: It will be necessary for one person to assume the responsibility of course coordination. This job will require the scheduling of teachers, students, teaching activities, assessment time and resources.

Allocation of time: Many courses are over-ambitious and require far more time (often on the part of students) for their completion than is reasonable. This is especially true of parts of a larger course of study. In allocating time, you will need to consider the total time available and its breakdown, and how time is to be spent in the course. It is often desirable to use blocks of time to deal with a particular topic, rather than 'spinning it out' over a term, semester or year.

Allocation of teaching rooms, laboratories and equipment: Courses depend for their success on the careful allocation of resources. Allocative procedures vary, but it is important that all competing claims are settled early so that orderly teaching can take place.

Technical and administrative support: Whether you teach a course alone, or as one of a team, you will find a need for support of some kind or other. It may be as simple as the services of someone to prepare course notes and examination papers, or as complex as requiring, at different times, the assistance of technicians. Your needs for support must be considered at the planning stage.

EVALUATING THE COURSE

Many teachers may find a discussion of course evaluation in a chapter on planning rather odd, perhaps believing that this activity is something that takes place **after** a course has been completed. We believe that this generally should not be the case. It is our contention that in teaching you should be progressively evaluating what you are doing and how the course design and plans are working out in practice. In this way, modifications and adjustments can be made in a planned and informed manner. But what is evaluation? You will often find the terms 'evaluation' and 'assessment' used interchangeably, but evaluation is generally understood to refer to the process of obtaining information about a course (or teaching) for subsequent judgement and decision-making. This process, properly done, will involve you in rather more than handing around a student questionnaire during the last lecture. What you do clearly depends on what you want to find out, but thorough course planning and course revision will require information about three different aspects of your course. These are the context of and inputs into your course, the processes of teaching, learning, assessment and course administration and, finally, the outcomes of the course.

Context and input evaluation: This is crucial if mistakes and problems are not to be attributed, unfairly, to teachers. In this type of evaluation you will need to consider the course in relation to such matters as other related courses, the entering abilities and characteristics of students, the resources and equipment available to teach with, and the overall design and planning arrangements for the course. The major sources of information you can use here will be in the form of course documents, student records, financial statements and the like.

Process evaluation: This focuses on the conduct of the teaching, learning, assessment and administration. It is here that the views of students can be sought as they are the only people who experience the full impact of teaching in the course. Questionnaires, written statements, interviews and discussion are techniques that you can consider.

Outcome evaluation: This looks at student attainments at the end of the course. Naturally you will review the results of assessment and judge whether they meet with the implied and expressed hopes for the course. Discussion with students and observation of aspects of their behaviour will help you determine their attitudes to the course you have taught.

In all evaluations, whether of a course or of teaching, it is helpful to keep in mind that there are many sources of information available to you and a variety of methods you can use. We suggest that you look at Chapter 10 on evaluation for more information about this.

GUIDED READING

For a useful extension of the material in this chapter we suggest you have a look at Susan Toohey's *Designing Courses for Higher Education* (SRHE and Open University Press, Buckingham, 1999) and John Biggs' *Teaching for Quality Learning at University: What the student does* (SRHE and Open University Press, Buckingham, 1999).

Chapter 9   Assessing the Students

INTRODUCTION

Being involved in student assessment is among the most critical of all tasks facing the teacher. Generally, teachers take such involvement quite seriously but, sadly, the quality of many assessment and examination procedures leaves much to be desired. The aim of this chapter, therefore, will be to help you to ensure that the assessments with which you are involved do what they are supposed to do in a fair and accurate way. We will provide some background information about the purposes of assessment and the basic principles of education measurement. We will then detail the forms of assessment with which you should be familiar in order that you can select an appropriate method.

THE PURPOSE OF ASSESSMENT

When faced with developing an assessment you must be quite clear about its purpose. This may appear to be stating the obvious but try asking your colleagues what they think is the purpose of the assessment with which you are concerned. We are certain that there will be a considerable diversity of opinion. Some may see it as testing the students' mastery of the course content, others may see it as a way of ranking the students, and yet others as a way of encouraging and supporting student learning.

Several purposes of assessment may be described as follows:

- judging mastery of essential skills and knowledge;
- measuring improvement over time;
- diagnosing student difficulties;
- providing feedback for students;
- evaluating the effectiveness of the course;
- motivating students to study.

Though it may be possible for one assessment method to achieve more than one of these purposes, all too often assessments are used for inappropriate purposes and consequently fail to provide valid and reliable data.

It must never be forgotten how powerfully an assessment affects students, particularly if it is one on which their future may depend. This influence may be positive or negative and even harmful. For many students, passing the examination at the end of the course is their primary motivation. Should this examination not be valid, and thus not truly reflect the content and objectives of the course, then the potential for serious distortions in learning and for making errors of judgement about students is evident. An example from our own experience may illustrate this point. A revision of the final-year medical curriculum inadvertently led to the multiple-choice test component of the end-of-year assessment having considerably more weight than the clinical component. Students were observed to be spending excessive amounts of time studying the theoretical aspects of the course in preference to practising their clinical skills, the latter being the main aim of the curriculum revision. A subsequent modification of the assessment scheme, giving equal weighting to an assessment of clinical competence, has corrected this unsatisfactory state of affairs.

It is our view that assessments can be of two broad kinds: those on which decisions about the students' future are to be made (summative assessment) and those which are for the benefit of the students in terms of guiding their further study (formative assessment).

Summative assessment

In dealing with summative assessment, every effort must be made to ensure that all assessments are fair and based on appropriate criteria. Students should be fully informed of these criteria, on the assessment methods to be employed and on the weightings to be given to each component. Such information should be given to students when a course begins. This is important because it is surprising how often information obtained from other sources, such as past students or even from the department itself, can be inaccurate, misleading or misinterpreted by the students. The best way of avoiding this is to provide printed details of the course plan, including the assessment scheme. Examples of past papers can be provided and we have found an open forum on the assessment scheme early in the course to be both popular and valuable.

Formative assessment

Formative assessments are generally undertaken on a continuous basis. Such assessments must be free of threat, as the aim is to get the students to reveal their strengths and weaknesses rather than to disguise them. Opportunities to obtain feedback on knowledge or performance are always appreciated by students and can lead to positive feelings about the department and the staff concerned.

WHAT YOU SHOULD KNOW ABOUT EDUCATIONAL MEASUREMENT

Whatever the purpose of the assessment, the method used should satisfy the following four requirements:

1 **Validity:** Does it measure what it is supposed to measure?

2 **Reliability:** Does it produce consistent results?

3 **Practicality:** Is it practical in terms of time and resources?

4 **Positive impact on learning**.

Our intention in raising these requirements is to encourage you to apply the same critical interest in the quality of educational assessment as you undoubtedly apply to the quality of your research. This section will provide you with some basic information about aspects of educational measurement with which we think you should be familiar.

Validity

Content validity is the first priority of any assessment. It is a measure of the degree to which the assessment contains a representative sample of the material taught in the course. A numerical value cannot be placed against it and it must be judged according to the objectives of the assessment. Therefore, in approaching any assessment the first question you must ask is: **what are the objectives of the course**?

Unfortunately, such objectives are not always available. Should you be in this situation, with no written objectives for the assessment you have to design, then you have no alternative but to develop them. This is not such a difficult task as you might imagine because, as far as the assessment is concerned, the objectives are embodied in the course content. A look at the teaching programme, lecture and tutorial topics, and discussions with teaching staff should allow you to identify and categorize the key features of the course. What you are, in fact, attempting to do is to construct a course plan in reverse and you may find it helpful at this point to consult Chapter 8 on curriculum planning where this process is discussed in greater detail.

The objectives of the course are the framework against which you can evaluate the content validity. For the content validity to be high, the assessment must sample the students' abilities **on each objective**. As these objectives are likely to cover a wide range of knowledge, skills and attitudes, it will immediately become apparent that no single test method is likely to provide a valid assessment. For instance, an essay test will hardly be likely to provide valid information about practical laboratory skills.

Other forms of validity exist but generally speaking you will not be in a position to evaluate them so they will not be discussed further. If you are interested, you should consult the guided reading at the end of the chapter.

Reliability

The reliability of any assessment is a measure of the consistency and precision with which it tests what it is supposed to test. Though its importance is initially less vital than validity, you should remember that an unreliable assessment cannot be valid. The degree of reliability varies with the assessment format itself, the quality of its administration and the marking.

Theoretically, a reliable assessment should produce the same result if administered to the same student on two separate occasions. Various methods are available which provide statistical indices of reliability and you should seek expert advice on these.

Another key component in determining the reliability of an assessment is the **consistency of the marking**. The absence of consistency is a major reason for the unacceptable levels of reliability in most forms of direct assessment and of written tests of the essay type. However, methods are available to help you minimize this problem and these will be discussed later in this chapter.

Improving validity and reliability of assessments

Validity can be improved by:

- carefully matching an assessment with the learning objectives, content and teaching methods;
- increasing the sample of objectives and content areas included in any given assessment;
- using methods that are appropriate for the objectives specified;
- employing a range of methods;
- ensuring adequate security and supervision to avoid cheating in examinations;
- improving the reliability of the assessment.

Reliability can be improved by:

- ensuring that questions are clear and suitable for the level of the students;
- checking to make sure time limits are realistic;
- writing instructions that are simple, clear and unambiguous;
- developing a marking scheme of high quality (eg explicit and agreed criteria, checking of marks, several skilled markers);
- keeping choices within a test paper to a minimum;
- when using less reliable methods, increasing the number of questions, observations or examination time.

Practicality

An assessment scheme must be practical. You may decide to use a scheme that is potentially highly valid and reliable but find that it is not practical to do so in your circumstances. Some questions you might consider here are:

- Do I have the skills to administer, mark and grade the assessment?
- Can I interpret the results accurately?

● Will the assessment scheme demand too much time?
● Does the scheme require special resources (eg labour, materials or equipment) and are these readily available to me?

Obviously, there will be other considerations of a practical nature that are peculiar to your own circumstances and that you will have to consider before implementing any particular scheme.

Norm-referenced versus criterion-referenced assessment

Before we finish dealing with some of the basic principles of educational measurement, we wish to introduce the difference between norm- and criterion-referenced assessment. You are likely to be familiar with norm-referenced assessment, as this reflects the traditional approach to testing. Any assessment which uses the results of all the students to determine the standard is of this type. In such tests the pass level is often determined arbitrarily, by predetermining the proportion of students given each grade, or 'grading the curve', as it is often called.

This traditional approach is one that we urge you to move away from. Some assumptions made are not appropriate to assessing learning in universities, and the approach can be shown to lack an educational justification. For example, do we seriously set out in our teaching to ensure that, no matter how well students achieve the objectives, because of our grading on the curve policy, some will fail? Surely, our task is to help all students to achieve the objectives and reduce gaps between them rather than getting a 'spread of scores'. We refer you to Biggs to understand this concept more fully.

It is necessary that the students achieve some minimal standard of competence. In this case, the criterion-referenced approach is more appropriate. Such an approach necessitates the determination of the standard before administering the assessment, rather than waiting to see the overall results before doing so. Though this can be difficult to implement, we have found that attempting to do so is a powerful way of improving the validity of the assessment. Everyone concerned is forced to consider each item in the assessment and ask themselves if it is relevant and set at the appropriate level of difficulty. Our own experiences with such an approach used to test clinical competence in the final year of the medical degree have been very revealing and rewarding.

Positive impact on learning

It is clear that how and what students learn is influenced more by our assessment practices than by any other factor in the curriculum. This influence is exerted at two levels. At a policy level, an over-emphasis on formal examinations and the implicit threat that this may carry will have a negative impact. At a methodological level, an emphasis on objective tests such as true/false and multiple-choice will almost certainly encourage and reward the use of surface learning strategies by students rather than approaches that demand higher-level intellectual processes such as reasoning and analysis. On the other hand, there are several assessment practices that can encourage and reward the kinds of learning that are more highly valued today. These approaches include essays, learning portfolios, research projects, self and peer assessment, and regular and constructive feedback on learning.

If we appreciate this influence, then we have a solution to the problem. In the criterion-referenced approach described above, the objectives are embedded in the assessment tasks, so if students focus on assessment, they will be learning what the objectives say they should be learning. This is a positive solution to the common problem of the negative impact of assessment.

ASSESSMENT METHODS

In planning your assessment, it is necessary to be aware of the variety of methods available to you. It is impossible to be comprehensive for reasons of space so we will restrict ourselves to some common methods. We will also include information about some innovative approaches developed recently which may be of interest. We do this deliberately in an attempt to encourage you to become subversive! With your new-found knowledge of assessment you will soon be involved in situations where it is obvious that inappropriate methods are being used. This may be due to a combination of tradition, ignorance and prejudice. The first two you may be able to influence by rational argument based on the type of information we provide in this book. The last is a more difficult problem with which to deal.

TYPES OF ASSESSMENT

1 Essay

2 Short-answer and simple computation questions

3 Objective tests

4 Direct observation

5 Oral

6 Structured practical assessment

7 Self assessment

8 The learning portfolio

1. ESSAY

We suggest caution in the use of the essay, except in situations where its unique attributes are required. The essay is the only means we have to assess students' ability to compose an answer and present it in effective prose. It can also indirectly measure attitudes, values and opinions. There are other reasons for the continuing popularity of essays. Of particular importance in higher education seem to be the assumptions that the production of written language and the expression of thought are scholarly activities of considerable worth and that essays encourage students to develop more desirable study habits.

Though they are relatively easy to set, essays are time-consuming to mark. The widespread use of multiple-choice tests and the advent of computer-scoring has lifted the marking burden from many academics, few of whom would wish to take it up again. Excluding such selfish reasons, there are other grounds for caution with essays. The most important is the potential for unreliable marking. Several studies have shown significant differences between the marks allocated by different examiners and even by the same examiner re-marking the same papers at a later date!

Essay questions tend to be of two kinds. The first is the **extended response**. An example is seen in Figure 9.1.

FIGURE 9.1 EXAMPLE OF
EXTENDED RESPONSE
ESSAY QUESTION

> Compare and contrast essay tests with objective tests in higher education.

In the extended response question the student's factual knowledge and ability to provide and organize ideas, to substantiate them and to present them in coherent English are tested. The extended essay is useful for testing knowledge objectives at the higher levels.

Another type of essay question is the **restricted response**, an example of which is shown in Figure 9.2. The restricted response form sets explicit boundaries on the answer required and on its organization.

FIGURE 9.2   *EXAMPLE OF
RESTRICTED RESPONSE
ESSAY QUESTION*

Explain the advantages and disadvantages of essay tests and objective tests in higher education with reference to:

1. validity; and
2. reliability.

This type of essay is best used for testing lower-level knowledge objectives. An advantage of the more restricted format is that it can decrease the scoring problems (and hence be more reliable).

Essays can be constructed in ways that – in theory at least – can test different levels of intellectual processes. Three simple examples are given:

Recall of basic principles

Describe the four basic requirements that must be met by an assessment method.

Analysis

Why is there so much dissatisfaction with examinations?

Evaluation

'We cannot have real learning in school if we think it is our duty and right to tell children what they must learn.' (John Holt). *Either* criticize *or* defend this statement.

If you intend to set and mark essay questions in an examination, then we suggest that you keep in mind the points in Figure 9.3.

For essays, or other written assignments required during a course of study, you can also take steps to improve the quality of feedback to students. One way is to use an

FIGURE 9.3 PROCEDURE FOR SETTING AND MARKING ESSAY QUESTIONS

Procedure

A Write questions that elicit the type of response suggested by the objectives.

Use clear directive words such as 'describe', 'compare', 'contrast', 'criticize' and 'explain'. If 'discuss' is used, be sure to indicate what points should be discussed.

Establish a clear framework which aims the student to the desired response. Rather than: 'Discuss small group teaching' try: 'Describe the educational benefits to be derived by including a programme of small group teaching in a course of study'.

B Set more questions requiring shorter answers of about a page, rather than a few questions requiring long answers.

This will provide a better sampling of course content, will reduce bias in marking for quantity rather than quality, and will improve reliability.

C Ensure that all students are required to answer the same or equivalent questions.

Constructing optional questions of equal difficulty is hard and, further you will not be able to make valid comparisons among students if they have answered questions that are not equivalent.

D Prepare a marking system.

Two methods are commonly used, both of which require you to prepare a model answer. In the **analytical method** of marking, a checklist of specific points is prepared against which marks are allocated. Such factors as 'logical argument' or 'expression' should be included if you think they are relevant. If you wish to reward legibility and presentation, give these components a proportion of the marks but avoid these aspects unduly biasing your assessment of the content. The **global method** of marking can be used if you have at least 30 papers to mark. Papers are read rapidly and assigned to one of five or more piles, grading from a superior response down to the inferior. Papers are then reread to check the original sorting. This is a faster and more reliable method of marking once standards for the various piles have been established.

E Mark questions with the following points in mind:

Mark anonymously.
Mark only one question at a time or, preferably, have a separate marker for each question.
Adopt consistent standards.
Try to mark each question without interruption.
Preferably have two independent markers for each question and average the result, or at least reread a sample of papers to check marking consistency.

assignment attachment of the kind shown in Figure 9.4, remembering that this particular form was designed for a specific course and should be adapted for your own specific needs.

Not only can this attachment provide very useful individual feedback, but used early in a course with a model answer, it can show students the standards you expect from them, and also help you in awarding marks.

FIGURE 9.4 AN ASSIGNMENT
ATTACHMENT

ASSIGNMENT ATTACHMENT

Prepared with the assistance of Educational Services & Teaching Resources Unit Murdoch University

Student's name: Assignment grade:

Itemised Rating Scale

(ticked *when applicable*)

←   →

STRUCTURE

Essay relevant to topic	Essay has little relevance
Topic covered in depth	Superficial treatment of topic

ARGUMENT

Accurate presentation of evidence	Much evidence inaccurate or questionable
Logically developed argument	Essay rambles & lacks continuity
Original & creative thought	Little evidence of originality

STYLE

Fluent piece of writing	Clumsily written
Succinct writing	Unnecessarily repetitive

PRESENTATION

Legible & well set out work	Untidy & difficult to read
Reasonable length	Over/under length

SOURCES

Adequate acknowledgement of sources	Inadequate acknowledgement of sources
Correct citation of references	Incorrect referencing

MECHANICS

Grammatical sentences	Several ungrammatical sentences
Correct spelling throughout	Much incorrect spelling
Effective use of figures & tables	Figures & tables add little to argument
Correct use of units & quantities	Some units incorrect

Please turn over

NOTES

- Sections left blank are not relevant to this assignment

- Some aspects are more important than others, so there is no formula connecting the number of ticks in different boxes with the grade.

- Key to grades:

  A An outstanding piece of work

  B Very good

  C Satisfactory

  D Generally unsatisfactory

  F Inadequate in most respects

- A tick in the left-hand box means that the statement on the left is true: a tick in the second box from the left means that the statement on the left is true to some extent. Similarly for the right-hand boxes, e.g.

Topic covered in depth | | | ✔ | | Superficial treatment of topic

means that the topic was treated somewhat superficially in the assignment.

- Ticks in the right hand boxes show areas of deficiency in the report.

EXPLANATION AND COMMENTS:

Tutor

2. SHORT-ANSWER AND SIMPLE COMPUTATION QUESTIONS

Short-answer tests have been surprisingly little used in recent years, yet another casualty of the multiple-choice boom. However, we have found them increasingly useful as our concerns about the limitations of the objective type have become more apparent.

Though easy to mark, it is essential that markers are provided with a well-constructed marking key, especially if more than one correct answer is possible, or if several processes are involved in answering the question. (See Figure 9.5.)

FIGURE 9.5   EXAMPLE OF A SIMPLE SHORT-ANSWER QUESTION WITH ANSWER KEY

> How many consonants are there in the word
> **AUSTRALIA?**
>
> Answer: 4 (one mark)

Clarifying the marking key is critical. In a very simple exercise that we conduct in our assessment workshops, we find that a group of markers will invariably give the piece of work shown in Figure 9.6 a mark ranging from 0 to 10 out of a maximum of 10!

FIGURE 9.6   WORKSHOP EXERCISE

> A student has worked out the following problem:
>
> $$269 \times$$
> $$\underline{23}$$
> $$787$$
> $$\underline{5380}$$
> $$\underline{6167}$$
>
> Working individually, give this student a mark out of ten

Those awarding zero argue that the answer is wrong and that wrong mathematical answers deserve zero. Those awarding other marks argue that substantial parts of the working are correct and deserve a proportion of the marks. However, all markers rapidly appreciate the importance of establishing marking guidelines to overcome this obvious problem of unreliable marking – even for an apparently straightforward piece of work!

Obviously more short-answer questions than essays can be fitted into a fixed time period. If one of the purposes of the assessment is to cover a wide content area, then short-answer questions have distinct advantages. Much of the same may be said about multiple-choice questions but short-answer questions have the advantage of avoiding cuing and requiring students to supply an answer, rather than to select or to guess from a fixed number of options. The major limitation of the short-answer test is that it is not suitable for testing complex learning outcomes.

If you wish to employ short-answer questions you should take account of the points in Figure 9.7.

FIG 9.7 PROCEDURE FOR SETTING AND MARKING SHORT-ANSWER QUESTIONS

A **Make the questions precise**

Direct questions are better than incomplete statements.

If a numerical answer is required, indicate the units and degree of precision required.

B **Prepare a structured marking sheet**

Allocate marks or part-marks for the acceptable answer(s).

Be prepared to consider other equally acceptable answers, some of which you may not have predicted.

C **Mark questions with the following points in mind:**

Mark anonymously.

Complete the marking of one page of questions at a time.

Preferably have a different examiner for each page of questions.

3. OBJECTIVE TESTS

This generic term is used in education to include a variety of test formats in which the marking of the answers is objective. Some classifications include short-answer questions in this category. The term multiple-choice test is sometimes used synonymously with the term objective test. However, we encourage you to use the more general term 'objective tests' as it allows us to include a wide variety of test types, only one of which can be accurately described as 'multiple-choice'. Other commonly used examples of objective tests are the true-false and matching types.

The characteristics of such tests are the high reliability of the scoring, the rapidity of scoring and economy of staff time in this task, and the ability to test large content areas. They lend themselves to the development of banks of questions, thus further reducing the time of examination preparation in the long term. These advantages have sometimes led to an over-reliance on objective tests and a failure to be critical in their use.

Considerable skill is required to write objective tests that measure higher-level intellectual skills.

In many disciplines, especially in the sciences and technologies, it is almost certain that you will have to participate in some way in writing or administering objective tests.

Choosing the type of question

You must find out or decide which type of item you will be using. Objective items, as we have said before, can be classified into three groups: **true–false**, **multiple-choice** and **matching**. We would suggest you stick to the true–false and multiple-choice types and avoid the more complex matching types which, in some examinations, often seem to behave more like tests of reading ability, rather than tests of the course content! For a variety of technical reasons, experts favour multiple-choice over other types of objective items.

True–false questions

Examples of true–false questions are shown in Figure 9.8 and 9.9.

FIGURE 9.8 EXAMPLE OF SIMPLE TRUE–FALSE ITEM

T	F	In a normal distribution the median, mode and mean coincide

FIGURE 9.9 EXAMPLE OF MULTIPLE (CLUSTER) TRUE–FALSE ITEM

In a 40 year-old patient with mild hypertension you would consider commencing treatment with

T	F	Atenolol
T	F	Methyldopa
T	F	Bendrofluazide
T	F	Nifedipine
T	F	Captopril

The **simple type** will obviously cause you the least problems in construction and scoring. The more complex **multiple type** (also known as the cluster type) is very popular because it allows a series of questions to be asked relating to a single stem or topic. Each question may be marked as a separate question. However, the questions may also be considered as a group with full marks given only if all the questions are correct and part-marks given if varying proportions of the questions are correct. Research has shown that the ranking of students is unaltered by the marking scheme used, so simplicity should be the guiding principle.

If you intend to use true–false questions you should take particular note of the points listed in Figure 9.10.

FIG 9.10 PROCEDURE FOR SETTING TRUE–FALSE QUESTIONS

Procedure

A Make sure that the content of the question is important and relevant and that the standard is appropriate to the group being tested.

B Use statements which are short, unambiguous and contain only one idea.

C Ensure that the statement is indeed unequivocally true or false.

D Avoid words which are give-aways to the correct answer, such as sometimes, always or never.

E Make sure that true statements and false statements are the same length and are written in approximately equal numbers.

F Avoid negative or double-negative statements.

Multiple-choice questions

An example of a simple multiple-choice questions (MCQ) is shown in Figure 9.11

FIG 9.11   EXAMPLE OF A SIMPLE MULTIPLE-CHOICE ITEM (ADAPTED FROM BLOOM AT AL)

'New criticism' is *most often* associated with which of the following pairs of terms?

1.   Ambiguity and paradox
2.   Comedy and tragedy
3.   Fear and pity
4.   Myth and symbol

The MCQ illustrated is made up of a stem (New criticism ... pairs of terms?) and four alternative answers. Of these alternatives one is correct and the others are known as 'distractors'.

One advantage of the MCQ over the true–false question is a reduction in the influence of guessing. Obviously, in a simple true–false question there is a 50 per cent chance of guessing the correct answer. In a one from four MCQ there is only a 25 per cent chance of doing so if all the distractors are working effectively. Unfortunately it is hard to achieve this ideal and exam-wise students may easily be able to eliminate one or two distractors and thus reduce the number of options from which they have to guess. Information about the effectiveness of the distractors is usually available after the examination if it has been computer-marked. Some advocate the use of correction formulas for guessing but this does not – on balance – appear to be worth the effort.

If you intend to use multiple-choice questions you should take particular note of the points in Figure 9.12.

Context-dependent questions

Having mastered the basic principles of setting good MCQ items, you may wish to become more adventurous. It is possible to develop questions with a more complex stem which may require a degree of analysis before the answer is chosen. Such items are sometimes known as context-dependent multiple-choice questions. One or

FIGURE 9.12   PROCEDURE FOR SETTING MULTIPLE-CHOICE QUESTIONS

Procedure

A Make sure that the content of the question is important and relevant and that the standard is appropriate to the group being tested.

B The main content of the question should be in the stem and the alternatives should be kept as short as possible.

C Eliminate redundant information from the stem.

D Ensure that each distractor is a plausible answer which cannot be eliminated from consideration because it is irrelevant or silly.

E Avoid giving clues to correct or incorrect responses which have nothing to do with the content of the question by:

- making sure correct and incorrect responses are of similar length;
- checking the grammar, particularly when the alternative is written as the completion of a statement in the stem;
- distributing the place of the correct response equally among positions 1 to 5 (or 1 to 4 as the case may be);
- avoiding 'always' or 'never'.

F Generally avoid 'all of the above' or 'none of the above' as alternatives.

G Avoid negatives.

H Do not try to write trick questions. For technical reasons use at least four alternative answers. Five are preferable but are more difficult to prepare.

more multiple-choice questions are based on stimulus material which may be presented in the form of a diagram, a graph, a table of data, a statement from a text or research report, a photograph and so on. This approach is useful if one wishes to attempt to test the student's ability at a higher intellectual level than simple recognition and recall of factual information.

Extended-matching questions

The extended-matching question (EMQ) is a development of the older matching item format, which tended towards testing lower-level intellectual skills such as recall. An example of an EMQ from the scientific study of nutrition is given in Figure 9.13.

FIGURE 9.13   EXAMPLE OF AN EXTENDED-MATCHING QUESTION (ADAPTED FROM CASE AND SWANSON)

Theme: Metabolic abnormalities

Options:
A.	Vitamin A	I.	Biotin
B.	Vitamin B1	J.	Copper
C.	Vitamin B2	K.	Folate
D.	Vitamin B6	L.	Iodine
E.	Vitamin C	M.	Iron
F.	Vitamin D	N.	Magnesium
G.	Vitamin E	O.	Niacin
H.	Vitamin K	P.	Zinc

Lead-in: For each patient with clinical features caused by metabolic abnormalities, select the vitamin or mineral that is most likely to be involved.

Stems:
1. A 70-year-old widower has ecchymoses, perifollicular petechiae, and swelling of the gingiva. His diet consists mostly of cola and hot dogs. (Answer: E)
2. Involved in clotting factor synthesis. (Answer: H)

The EMQ is typically made up of four parts: a theme of related concepts, a list of options, lead-in statement to direct students and two or more item stems. EMQs can be useful in diagnostic-type situations or for testing management decision making.

The item shown includes two item stems that illustrate how this EMQ might test at different intellectual levels. The first stem requires problem solving in order to determine a diagnosis; the second stem tests only recall. More stems could, of course, be added to this example to increase the content coverage of the test item and the range of levels tested. In some respects, EMQs share similarities with the context-dependent MCQ we described earlier: the option list (provided it is always longer than the number of stems to reduce the impact of cueing) is a rich resource for developing more stems EMQs are also relatively easy to write compared to MCQs.

FIGURE 9.14 *PROCEDURE FOR SETTING EXTENDED-MATCHING ITEMS (AFTER CASE AND SWANSON)*

Procedure

A Identify the theme for the set of EMQ's.

B Write the lead-in for the set to indicate the relationship between the stems and options and to clearly state the question posed for students.

C Prepare the list of options. The list should be single words or short phrases presented in alphabetical order unless there is some logical order that should be maintained. As always, avoid 'tricks' in the list and in the items.

D Write the items. Often, short word-pictures of a situation are appropriate. A rich source can be your own professional practice of your discipline.

E Review the items, checking to make sure that there is only a single best answer for each question and that there are at least four reasonable distractors for each item in the options list. As with all test item writing, it is a good idea to ask a colleague to review the questions you have prepared, and even better if you can form a team to write and review questions.

Putting together an objective test

This is the point where many tests come to grief. It is not enough simply to select 100 questions from the item bank or from among those recently prepared by your colleagues. The selection must be done with great care and must be based on the objectives of the course. A blueprint, or table of test specifications should be prepared which identifies the key topics of the course which must be tested. The number of questions to be allocated to each topic should then be determined according to its relative importance. Once this is done the job becomes easier. Sort out the objective items into the topics and select those which cover as many areas within the topic as possible. It is advisable to have a small working group at this stage to check the quality of the questions and to avoid your personal bias in the selection process. You may find that there are some topics for which there is an inadequate number or variety of questions. You should then commission the writing of additional items from appropriate colleagues or, if time is short, your committee may have to undertake this task.

The questions should now be put in order. It is less confusing to students if the items for each topic are kept together. Check to see that the correct answers are randomly distributed throughout the paper and, if not, re-order accordingly. Deliver the paper to the secretary for typing, with suitable instructions about the format required and the need for security. At the same time make sure that the 'Instructions to Students' section at the beginning of the paper is clear and accurate. Check and recheck the typed copy as errors are almost invariably discovered during the examination, a cause of much consternation. Finally, have the paper printed and arrange for secure storage until the time of the examination.

Scoring and analyzing an objective test

The main advantage of the objective type tests is the rapidity with which scoring can be done. This requires some attention to the manner in which the students are to answer the questions. It is not usually appropriate to have the students mark their answers on the paper itself. When large numbers are involved, a separate structured sheet should be used. Where facilities are available it is convenient to use answer sheets that can be directly scored by computer or for responses to be entered directly into a computer by students. However, a hand-marking answer sheet can easily be prepared. An overlay is produced by cutting out the positions of the correct responses. This can then be placed over the student's answer sheet and the correct responses are easily and rapidly counted. Before doing so ensure that the student has not marked more than one correct answer!

There are several analytic techniques that you can use with objective test scores. We suggest that you have one of the books listed at the end of the chapter, such as Mehrens and Lehman, beside you when you undertake this task.

4. DIRECT OBSERVATION

Direct observation of the student performing a technical or an interpersonal skill in the real, simulated or examination setting would appear to be the most valid way of assessing such skills. Unfortunately, the reliability of these observations is likely to be seriously low. This is particularly so in the complex interpersonal area where no alternative form of assessment is available. Nevertheless, in professional courses it is essential to continue to make assessments of the student's performance, if only to indicate to the student your commitment to these vital skills.

In doing so, you would be well advised to use the information predominantly for feedback rather than for important decision-making.

Various ways have been suggested by which these limitations might be minimized. One is to improve the method of scoring and another is to improve the performance of the observer. The former involves the design of checklists and rating forms.

Checklists

A checklist is basically a two-point rating scale. Evidence suggests that the reliability of a checklist decreases when there are more than four points on the scale. The assessor has to decide whether each component on the list is present/absent; adequate/inadequate; satisfactory/unsatisfactory. Only if each component is very clearly defined and readily observable can a checklist be reliable. They are particularly useful for assessing technical skills.

Rating forms

Rating forms come in many styles. The essential feature is that the observer is required to make a judgement along a scale which may be continuous or intermittent. They are widely used to assess behaviour or performance because no other methods are usually available, but the subjectivity of the assessment is an unavoidable problem. Because of this, multiple independent ratings of the same student undertaking the same activity are essential if any sort of justice is to be done. The examples in Figure 9.15 show several alternative structures for rating the same ability. They are derived from published formats used to obtain information about ward performance of trainee doctors. The component skill being assessed is 'Obtaining the data base' and only one subcomponent (obtaining information from the patient) is illustrated.

Format 3 is the one we would recommend for two reasons. The first is that there is an attempt to provide

FIGURE 9.15 EXAMPLES
OF RATING FORMS

Format 1

	Top quarter	Upper-middle quarter	Lower-middle quarter	Bottom quarter
Obtaining information from the patient	4	3	2	1

Format 2

Obtaining information from the patient

☐	☐	☐	☐	☐	☐
Very effective	Effective	Reasonable	Poor	Inadequate	Unable to judge

Format 3

Obtaining information from the patient

☐	☐	☐	☐
Little or no information obtained	Some information obtained; major errors or omissions	Adequate performance; most information elicited	Very thorough exploration of patient's problems

descriptive anchor points which may be helpful in clarifying for the observer what standards should be applied. The second is a more pragmatic one. In a study we undertook, it was the format most frequently preferred by experienced clinical raters.

Improving the performance of the observer

It has often been claimed that training of raters will improve reliability. This seems to make sense but what evidence there is shows that training makes remarkably little difference! A recent study of our own suggested that a better approach might be to select raters who are inherently more consistent than others. Common sense dictates that observers should be adequately briefed on the rating form and that they should not be asked to rate on aspects of the student's performance that they have not observed.

5. ORAL

The oral or viva-voce examination has for centuries been the predominant method, and sometimes the only method, used to assess medical students. The traditional oral, which gives considerable freedom to the examiner to vary the questions asked from student to student and to exercise personal bias, has consistently been shown to be very unreliable. One major study of oral examinations showed that the correlation between different examiners was overall no greater than would have occurred by chance! There is no reason to believe that oral examinations conducted in other disciplines would stand up any better to similar scrutiny.

Without doubt, face-to-face interaction between student and examiner provides a unique opportunity to test language and interactive skills which cannot be assessed in any other way. However, these skills are not usually the focus of attention and several studies have shown that the majority of questions in oral examinations require little more than the recall of isolated fragments of information, something more easily and more reliably assessed by objective written tests.

We would recommend that reliance on oral examination be considerably reduced unless, of course, it is obviously the only valid assessment method; for example, in the speaking of a foreign language or as a way of assessing a student with a disability. It might be possible to incorporate many of the activities currently assessed in oral examinations into the objective-structured approach discussed in the next section.

Should you wish to retain oral examinations then certain steps should be undertaken to minimize the likely problems, as outlined in Figure 9.16.

FIGURE 9.16 PROCEDURE FOR CONDUCTING ORAL EXAMINATIONS

Procedure

A Standardize the content

- Define the content to be tested.
- If it is a theoretical oral get the examiners together beforehand and prepare a standard set of questions to be asked of each student. These should be identical if examined students can be kept apart from students yet to be examined. If not, the questions should be equivalent in content and difficulty.
- If it is a practical test the same principles should apply but in this case the students should be faced with similar or equivalent situations and asked to perform the same tasks.

B Reduce examiner inconsistency

- Prepare structured marking sheets or rating forms and brief examiners in their use.
- Use as many examiners as possible. In other words, break down the oral examination into several shorter sessions rather than one long session.
- Ensure that each student gets asked the agreed questions and is given approximately the same time to answer them.
- Ensure that each examiner marks independently and avoids discussing individual students until all marks are collated.
- Establish controls for potential bias due to differences in student's and examiner's age, sex and ethnicity.

6. STRUCTURED PRACTICAL ASSESSMENT

In recent years there has been a search for new approaches to assessment. One of the most interesting of these developments has been the 'objective structured practical examination' described by Harden and Cairncross and subsequently developed by ourselves and others as an integral part of medical examinations. This approach to the assessment of practical skills has now been taken up by a variety of professions.

The structured examination is essentially an administrative structure into which a variety of test methods can be incorporated. The aim is to test a wide range of skills in an objective fashion.

The students proceed through a series of 'stations' and undertake a variety of practical tasks. Marking sheets and checklists are prepared beforehand to improve the reliability of scoring. All students are thus examined on the same content and marked on the same criteria by the same examiners. As in any form of assessment, the definition of the content to be tested and the preparation of good test items is essential if a high degree of validity and reliability are to be obtained.

Should you wish to consider introducing such an approach you should read the two articles given in the references and adapt the ideas to your own discipline.

7. SELF-ASSESSMENT

By 'self-assessment' we mean an assessment system which involves the students in establishing the criteria and standards they will apply to their work and then in making judgements about the degree to which they have been met.

We believe that the skill of being able to make realistic evaluations of the quality of one's work is one that every graduate should have. Yet, in conventional courses, few opportunities are provided for self-assessment skills to be learnt and developed.

The introduction of self-assessment practices into existing courses has been shown to be feasible and desirable. Whether marks generated in this way should count towards a final grade is an undecided issue, but one which is receiving attention in the literature. Work reported by Boud on self-assessment in student grading suggests that, so long as the assessment scheme is well designed and students grade themselves on achievement (and not effort), they will generate marks which are reasonably consistent with staff marks. Thus, there is little doubt that self-assessment, used primarily to improve the students' understanding of their own ability and performance, is worthwhile educationally and encourages openness and honesty about assessment.

If you wish to embark on a trial scheme you must first set about the task of establishing criteria and standards. This can be done at a series of small group meetings attended by staff and students. Both must agree on the criteria to be applied to the students' work. To help focus on this task you might have students reflect on questions such as:

How would you distinguish good from inadequate work? What would characterize a good assignment in this course?

Once criteria have been specified, students use them to judge their own performance. Marks are awarded with reference to each criterion and a statement justifying the mark should be included. An alternative is to contrast their own mark with one given to them by a peer. The teacher may also mark a random sample to establish controls and to discourage cheating or self-delusion. We urge you to give this approach to assessment very serious consideration indeed. In our view, it is among the most educationally promising ideas in recent years, and we suggest you study the book by Boud listed at the end of this chapter.

8. THE LEARNING PORTFOLIO

All assessment methods require that students present evidence of their learning, yet in most cases (with thesis and project work being notable exceptions) it is the teacher who controls the character of that evidence. Requiring students to respond to objective tests, write essays on designated topics, participate in orals or solve problem sets, for example, does this.

If we really believe in student-centred learning then we must work hard to ensure that our assessment practices reflect, encourage and reward this belief. In Chapter 2, we noted that assessment in student-centred learning needs to be more flexible with greater emphasis on student responsibility. The learning portfolio is one way of reinforcing student-centred learning. The portfolio clearly has validity as an assessment method in this situation, but its reliability for summative purposes has yet to be determined. This should not, however, discourage you from experimenting with learning portfolios with your students.

A learning portfolio is a collection of evidence presented by students to demonstrate what learning has taken place. In the portfolio, the student assembles, presents, explains and evaluates his or her learning in relation to the objectives of the course and his or her own purposes and goals. Used for many years in disciplines like the fine arts and architecture, portfolios are now being used more widely.

A learning portfolio might have several parts, such as:

- An introductory statement defining what the objectives are and what the student hopes to accomplish.
- A presentation of items of evidence to show what learning has taken place.
- An explanation of why items are chosen and presented, evidence of the application of learning to some issue or real-life situation, and an evaluation of learning outcomes.

A danger of using portfolios is that students might do too much, and some of their material might be less than relevant! So it is important to provide structure and to suggest sample items, the number of different items and their approximate size. Obviously, the items in a portfolio will reflect your particular discipline. Some ideas are listed in Figure 9.17.

FIGURE 9.17   POSSIBLE CONTENT FOR A LEARNING PORTFOLIO

- An original essay, creative work, and project or fieldwork reports (perhaps some in note form).
- A concept map of the course or unit of study (see Figure 4.1 for a simple example).
- A brief report of a student research project or other learning activity carried out individually or with peers.
- Answers to some objective test items or problems, giving both the answer and an explanation as to why the answer is correct, and possibly comments on the test items themselves.
- A student publication relevant to the student's goals or the unit's objectives.
- An abstract of a book or journal article with an explanation as to why the reading was considered important.
- A taped interview with an expert, a patient, a client or another student.
- A set of questions, and a justification, that might form the basis of a test on the unit.

- A description of how materials and resources were used in learning (eg texts, libraries, other people, the Internet etc).
- An account of involvement in an activity, student association or society and how that involvement assisted with learning.
- A case study.
- A self or peer-assessed piece of work.
- Any item submitted and judged to be appropriate by the student.

Implementing learning portfolios as an assessment method requires careful preparation and planning on your part. In his discussion of portfolios, John Biggs recommends that most of the following should be considered, and we suggest you look at his book for more information on these matters:

- Clarify for students, perhaps in the unit's objectives, what the evidence for good learning might be.
- Specify the requirements for the learning portfolio in terms of:
  - the structure of the portfolio;
  - a list of sample items;
  - the number of items required (Biggs suggests that four is the maximum in a semester-length unit);
  - the size of items and the overall portfolio;
  - any required items.

Decide how the portfolio will be assessed. It is suggested that global assessment of the whole portfolio is preferred to analytical marking to ensure that the broader purposes of students reporting and evaluating their learning are preserved and not broken down into discrete elements.

ASSESSING STUDENTS WITH A DISABILITY

Institutions have implemented many policies and practices to assist students with a disability. Unfortunately, consideration of their special needs is not always extended to the assessment of their learning. It is good practice for staff in departments to review and share alternative assessment arrangements on a regular basis as such arrangements are likely to be specific to both the kind of disability and to the nature of the discipline.

You are not expected to lower academic standards to accommodate these students but rather to provide them with a reasonable and fair opportunity to demonstrate their learning. Thus, you may need to make adjustments to assessment tasks once you understand how the particular disability affects performance. Space does not allow us to go into all the possible options here, but the following suggestions for specific disabilities will give your students a more equal opportunity in your course. Common strategies will be to simply follow good assessment practices we have described elsewhere and to be flexible in your insistence on assignment deadlines and in the time allowed in formal examinations.

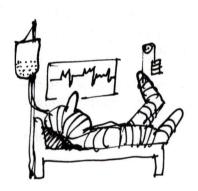

FIGURE 9.18
ASSESSMENT-
SUPPORT
STRATEGIES

Disability	Assessment – support strategy
Vision impairment:	provide a reader, an oral examination, audio-taped questions, or large-print papers
Hearing impairment:	provide someone to sign questions and instructions
Mobility disability:	allow students a combination of written and oral examination but allow students to plan their oral answers either verbally or in writing to assist in their spoken presentation

Medical disability:	allow take away examinations to allow students to be in a comfortable environment where support systems are available
Psychiatric or psychological disability:	postpone assessments when the disability enters an active phase; reduce anxieties by permitting tests to be undertaken privately away from perceived threats or distractions

ASSESSING STUDENTS AS GROUPS

With the increasing use of group and team-based learning in higher education there is the related challenge of assessing the outcomes of group learning in ways that are fair to individuals but which recognize the particular dynamics and realities of group learning. More detailed descriptions of this assessment approach are given in Miller, Imrie and Cox and in Brown and Glasner, but the following ideas will be helpful when assessing group assignments.

Preparatory matters are important. Remember to keep group size down (greater than six members is too large); help students to work as effective group members; form groups randomly and change membership at least each semester; and ensure all students understand the assessment mechanisms you will use to encourage the diligent and forewarn the lazy.

Marking group submissions can be a way of assessing more students but taking up less time on your part. When allocating marks, the following strategies will be helpful:

● Give all members of a group the same group mark where it was an objective to learn that group effectiveness is the outcome of the contribution of all.

● Give the group a mark to distribute as they determine. For example if the group report was given a mark of 60 per cent and there were 4 members, give the group 240 (4 × 60) to divide up. This will be best managed if you have forewarned the group and assisted them to develop written criteria at the outset as to how they will allocate marks. An alternative is to have members draw up a contract to undertake certain group responsibilities or components. Components may be marked separately, or students may be given the task of assessing contributions themselves.

● Enhance the reliability of this form of assessment by conducting short supplementary interviews with students (eg What was your contribution?, How did you reach this conclusion?, to gauge individual contribution and build project-related questions into any final examination (eg Describe how your group developed..., Using your group project as an example, how would you...?).

USING TECHNOLOGY IN ASSESSMENT

Computer technologies can be used to support assessment and we suggest you explore the facilities that are likely to be available to you in your own institution. There are a number of ways in which technology can be used. These include:

● As a management tool to store, distribute and analyse data and materials. An assessment system should be integrated with larger systems in your department or institution for curriculum management such as student data and course materials.

● As a tool in the assessment process. One way is for the marking and scoring of tests. Answers from objectives-type tests can be read by an optical mark reader and results processed by computer. However, more elaborate tools are now available to assess students' work directly. Software can be purchased that enables you to prepare, present and score tests and assignments. You should check to see if your institution has a licence for some of these software products.

● As a resource for student learning and assessment. Basically, this involves students using technology to prepare and present work for assessment. Some simple examples include students preparing essays using a word processor or completing tasks using a spreadsheet application and submitting their work via e-mail. E-mail can also be used to provide a mechanism for the all-important feedback process from the teacher or from other students if collaborative group work or peer assessment is being used.

We recognize that information technology and telecommunications can be helpful and positive tools or resources for assessment. But we also have serious reservations about the way technology is being used as a tool in the assessment process. This is because the technology is so well suited for the administration and scoring of objective-type tests of the multiple-choice or true/false kind. We are seeing something of a resurgence of this kind of assessment in higher education with all of the well-known negative influences this may have on learning when items are poorly constructed or test only recall. All we can do here is urge caution, use good-quality test items, and to always ensure that students receive helpful feedback on their learning.

FEEDBACK TO STUDENTS

Major purposes of assessing student learning are to diagnose difficulties and to provide students with feedback. Several approaches to doing this have already been identified in this chapter and some of the methods described readily lend themselves to providing opportunities for feedback. To be specific:

- use assignment attachments for feedback on essays (p 178);
- provide immediate feedback on technical, interpersonal, or oral skills as an outcome of direct observations, orals or practical assessments (pp 190–95); and
- use self-assessment which includes feedback as part of the process (pp 195–97).

Some guidelines for giving feedback include the following:

- keep the time short between what students do and the feedback;
- balance the positive with the negative;
- indicate how the student can improve;
- encourage students to evaluate themselves and give feedback to each other; and
- make the criteria clear when setting work and relate feedback to the criteria.

'Classroom Assessment Techniques' (CATs) are another way of providing feedback to students and incidentally a very positive strategy to provide learner activity and formative assessment in large lectures. One simple example of a CAT is the 'one-minute paper'. This requires students to, for example, write down the main idea discussed in the lecture and then pass their paper to the teacher. After scanning the papers the teacher is able to provide feedback and possibly supplementary teaching. The book by Angelo and Cross should be consulted for ideas.

REPORTING THE RESULTS OF ASSESSMENT

In many major examinations you will be required to report the results as a final mark or grade based on a number of different assessment methods. What usually happens is that marks from these different assessments are simply added or averaged and the final mark or grade awarded. Simple though this approach may be, it can introduce serious distortions. Factors contributing to this problem may be: differing distributions of marks in each subtest; varying numbers of questions; differing levels of difficulty; and a failure to appropriately weight each component.

The answer is to convert each raw subscore to a standardized score. This is not the place to do more than alert you to the need to do so and refer you to a text on educational measurement (eg Mehrens and Lehmann) or to advise you to enlist the aid of an educational statistician, who can usually be found by contacting the teaching unit in your institution.

GUIDED READING

There are many useful general texts on educational measurement. Two which provide straightforward accounts of the principles and procedures of assessment are: W A Mehrens and I J Lehmann's *Measurement and Evaluation in Education and Psychology* (4th Edn, Holt, Rinehart & Winston, New York, 1991); and N E Gronlund and R L Linn's *Measurement and Evaluation in Teaching* (Merril Press, Bellevue, Washington, 2000). Both have useful discussions of broad assessment considerations such as objectives, planning, reliability, validity and scoring, and also provide a wide range of examples of test items that you could use as models for your own tests.

Another book which you may find useful is the *Handbook on Formative and Summative Evaluation of Student Learning* by B S Bloom, J T Hastings and G F Madaus (McGraw-Hill, New York, 1971). This two-part volume is particularly useful for the development of test items and contains numerous examples designed to test achievement at different levels of Bloom's taxonomy of educational objectives. *Assessment Matters in Higher Education* by S Brown and A Glasner (SRHE and Open University

Press, Buckingham, 1999) is another general overview text that we recommend because of the many examples relevant to higher education.

We can also recommend *Student Assessment in Higher Education* by A H Miller, B W Imrie and K Cox (Kogan Page, London, 1998), *Assessing Student Learning in Higher Education* by George Brown *et al* (Routledge, London, 1997) and Chapter 9 of *Teaching for Quality Learning at University* by John Biggs (SRHE and Open University Press, Buckingham, 1999).

Books and articles referred to in this chapter:

Angelo, T A and Cross, K P (1993) *Classroom Assessment Technique: A handbook for college teachers*, Jossey-Bass, San Francisco.

Boud, David (1995) *Enhancing Learning Through Self Assessment*, Kogan Page, London.

Case, S M and Swanson, D B (1996) *Constructing Written Test Questions for the Basic and Clinical Sciences*, 2nd edn, National Board of Medical Examiners, Philadelphia. (Look at Chapter 6 of this book; it is available online at: www.nbme.org/new.version/item.htm)

Harden, R M and Cairncross, R G (1980) 'Assessment of practical skills: the objective structured practical examination (OSPE)' *Studies in Higher Education*, **5**, pp. 187–96.

Newble, D I (1988) 'Eight years' experience with a structured clinical examination' *Medical Education*, **22**, pp. 200–4.

Chapter 10   The Evaluation of Teaching and Learning

In this chapter, we want to help you do three important things:

- We want to provide you with information and resources that will assist you to evaluate your teaching and your students' learning.
- We want to guide you in ways that will assist you to make good use of the information you create through your evaluative activities.
- We want to arm you with ideas on how to improve the practice of evaluation in your institution.

The third point is especially important, and is often over-looked. In our experience, as many difficulties in evalua-tion are created by the implementation of poor policies and practices as by the processes of collecting and presenting evaluative information. One poor practice is an obsession with quantification. This has led to an over-emphasis of those things that can be most easily counted, such as students' ratings of a teacher's behaviour, and an under-emphasis of those areas of academic work less easy to quantify, such as learning processes or advising students.

There is another important factor here as well. Just as the ways in which we go about assessing our students will directly influence their learning behaviour, so too will the ways institutions evaluate their teachers, drive teachers' behaviour. For example, the strong emphasis on research in many universities is, in part, a direct consequence of the way we evaluate and reward academic activity by promoting people who may be competent researchers but poor teachers.

Before we address these matters in more detail, we want to outline the context in which we are presenting ideas to you and to clarify some important concepts.

THE CONTEXT OF EVALUATION

Evaluation and learning

In our Statement of Educational Principles, we identified evaluation as one of the key elements of effective learning and teaching. We said:

> A characteristic that is closely related to instruction is the assessment of student learning and the evaluation of teaching. Reliable and valid assessment of learning and giving helpful comments on students' work is a distinguishing characteristic of good teaching. So too is learning from students about the effects of teaching – their misunderstandings, their approaches to studying, and their perceptions of the course and what we do as teachers.

Evaluation is an important part of the process of learning – it is about learning from our students and their learning and learning about our teaching. How can we do this? We shall be suggesting some ideas about this after we have briefly reviewed another important side of evaluation: accountability.

Evaluation and accountability

One of the most dramatic shifts in higher-education practice in the past decade has been the move towards accountability. By 'accountability', we mean a demand to provide clear evidence of what is being done in higher education and of the outcomes of learning and teaching. This evidence is then used in a variety of ways, one of which of major interest to you is decisions about academic promotions and contracts.

At the national level, governments are generally under pressure to account for the way public funds are used, and so exert a corresponding pressure on institutions to improve their effectiveness. Owners and trustees exert similar pressures in the non-government sector of higher education. Institutions are thus required to gather data about learning and teaching and present it as evidence of their claims of effectiveness and quality.

Institutions, in turn, have exerted accountability demands on to faculties, teaching departments and individuals. They commonly require that courses be evaluated on a regular basis, and that teachers evaluate their teaching and use the information obtained for the improvement of teaching and courses, and also when making a case for contract renewal, promotion or tenure.

Evaluation: some definitions and principles

Evaluation is a process of obtaining information to form judgements and make decisions about programmes, courses and teachers. Assessment, a term that is sometimes used interchangeably with evaluation, is about obtaining information for judgement and decision making about students and their learning. However, the results of an assessment of student learning are a very important part of evaluation.

We are sure you will be familiar with some of the ways commonly used to gather information – questionnaires and interviews for teaching evaluations, and assignments and examinations for the assessment of student learning. Strategies for judgement and decision making are less well-developed, however, and we will look at these later in the chapter.

You should keep in mind two broad intentions behind evaluation. The first is 'formative evaluation'. This is intended to assist in change, development and improvement in teaching. The second is 'summative evaluation'.

This is used to make decisions such as whether to promote or reappoint a teacher.

Whatever the intentions of an evaluation, you will find it useful to keep in mind that there are several sources of evaluative information and methods you can use to get this information. These matters are summarized in Figure 10.1 and Figure 10.2.

FIGURE 10.1   SOURCES OF INFORMATION FOR AN EVAUATION

What are some sources for an evaluation of learning and teaching?	What are some examples of valid information they can give you?
People Sources	
Students	Course Implementation; teaching behaviours
Academic colleagues	Contribution to the administration of teaching
Graduates	Relationship of courses to work
Observers	Descriptions of what is occurring
Professional associations	Comparative data against some agreed standard
Self	Satisfaction; allocation of resources (time)
Administrators, Departmental Heads, Deans	Administration, commitment, innovation
Employers	Satisfaction with graduate skills
Material Sources	
Course materials	Teaching plans and philosophies, administration
Products of student learning and assessment results	Learning outcomes
Files/records	Administrative matters, student data

Different methods are available to gather information from these sources. For example, if you are particularly interested in a student's experiences, you may decide to use several different methods including diaries, questionnaires and focus groups. Some of these methods are listed in Figure 10.2.

Space does not allow us to explore all of these sources and methods, which of course can be used in a wide range of

FIGURE 10.2   METHODS AND
TECHNIQUES FOR AN EVALUATION

What are some methods of gathering information?	In what ways can these methods be used?
Questionnaires	Surveys of student, graduate, employer opinion
Interviews	In-depth exploration of issues
Students' diaries/work records/logs	Learning activities, processes and reaction
Discussion (focus groups, panels)	Identification of issues in teaching or courses
Comments (both solicited and unsolicited)	Student reaction to a broad range of issues
Observation of student/teacher behaviour	Learning processes; teaching behaviour
'Unobtrusive' observation (eg, noting the extent of use of recommended books)	Students' learning activities
Feedback sections on homepages attached to an e-mail address	Almost all areas of teaching and other facilities
Results of student work	Learning
Personally gathered information (teaching portfolio)	Documenting and describing teaching

combinations. For more help, we recommend you consult someone in your institution's teaching unit or review the references provided at the end of the chapter.

In deciding among the options in the table, you need to be aware that two fundamental characteristics of evaluation are validity and reliability. Other important characteristics are the practicality of an evaluation and, of course, its acceptability to all those involved.

Validity refers to the truthfulness and appropriateness of information provided as evidence of learning and teaching. For example, high levels of student achievement may not be a valid indicator of teaching competence because of the problem of identifying the relative contribution of teacher, the effort made by the student, library resources available, students' peers and so on. On the other hand, it is a valid indicator of learning. Students can provide valid feedback on the availability of resources and teacher behaviour, for example, because they observe and experience these things as part of their course.

Reliability refers to the extent to which the information provided is dependable and consistent. For example, information about a teacher based on the results of just one student survey will not be as reliable as information derived from several surveys conducted over several years and from a representative range of classes taught. The reliability of an evaluation may also be enhanced if different, but valid, methods are used in combination.

Now, armed with this background knowledge, how might you go about evaluating your teaching? There is one important preliminary matter to consider: planning.

Planning evaluation as part of your teaching

Among the things you need to think about are the following:

1. Determine what your institution's formal requirements for evaluation are. For example, is there a requirement that you should gather student feedback on a regular basis for curriculum development or for promotion or tenure?
2. Make contact with the staff of your teaching unit, who will at least be able to advise you if not provide direct evaluation services for you.
3. Draw up your own plan of evaluation. As we have already suggested, evaluation is an important element of good teaching, and so is something that you should be doing all the time.

Matters that you will need to consider in your plan are how and when you will evaluate your teaching, how you will evaluate student learning and what you will do with the information you gather. You must have some plan to use the information in ways to improve or develop learning and your teaching, otherwise there is little point in doing it at all. One way of using information will be to incorporate it into an ongoing record of your work known as a 'teaching portfolio', which we will explain below. Another important way of using information is to ensure that you give your students feedback on the outcomes of your evaluation and inform them what you plan to do with the results. Practical ways in which you can communicate this kind of information are through your personal or departmental Web page, or by posting information on the student notice board.

THE EVALUATION OF LEARNING AND TEACHING

Evaluating learning

As with all evaluation, the process of evaluating learning consists of two major elements: gathering information about learning, and then making judgements based upon that information. What sources of information are there about learning? The reliability of your evaluation of student learning will be enhanced by your judicious use of more than one valid measure of learning. So what is available?

The first, and major, source of information about student learning will be the results of your programme of student assessment – the examination and test results, assignments, projects, dissertations, field reports, clinical notes and other products and observations of student learning.

In our experience, a great deal of useful information from students is overlooked. For example, it is necessary to go beyond the scores and grades from tests and ask questions about *learning*; for example:

- What are common errors – and how can I address these in my teaching?
- In what areas have students shown particular strengths, weaknesses, interests – and why might this be so?

- What misconceptions are evident in students work – and how can I address these in my teaching?
- Am I satisfied with the quality of student writing – and how will I address this?
- What levels of intellectual achievement are revealed in students' work – for example, do they simply reflect reproductive learning or is there evidence of original analysis or creativity?
- What feedback will I give students and how will I do this? In lectures, via the Web, by posting a notice or in face-to-face meetings?

This process of questioning, reflecting, and follow-up is a fertile way of developing your understanding of student learning so that you can modify teaching or provide additional assistance to students if this is indicated as being needed.

The second way of evaluating learning is through well-designed and administered evaluations of teaching. There is a considerable body of research evidence that shows this to be a valid measure of teacher-mediated learning in students, provided that the questions ask about factors relating to learning and not something else! Information about how students are progressing in achieving the goals of your teaching can be found in questionnaire items such as:

- I have understood the concepts presented in the subject.
- I have a positive attitude to this subject.
- My ability to work independently has been increased.
- My ability to [think critically/solve problems/perform clinical tasks/etc] has increased.

Apart from formal questionnaire surveys, you will find that evaluation by brainstorming an issue with your students (such as, 'Are the course objectives being achieved?') or by using the evaluation discussion method described in Chapter 3 on small groups, can be a very powerful learning experience for all involved!

The third way you can obtain information about the processes of learning is by using tools such as CATs (Classroom Assessment Techniques). We have already described two CATs on page 75. These were the minute paper used to gather useful information on what, how much, and how well students are learning, and the pro-and-con grid, which both encourages and assesses thinking skills. You should refer to that material for an introduction to this useful tool.

Another CAT has been developed to help teachers to evaluate students' reactions to exams and tests and to improve these as effective learning and assessment devices. Called the 'exam evaluation', the procedure for using this evaluation tool is:

- Focus on a type of test you are going to use more than once.
- Develop questions that you would like to ask students. You might also consider asking *students* what questions they would like to be asked.
- Choose the questions and decide whether you will ask these at the end of a test or as part of a follow-up evaluation. Examples of questions are: 'Did you learn more from one type of test than another?' 'What is it about the test that accounts for this?' 'Was the test a fair assessment of your learning?' 'What are the reasons for your response?'.

In their book *Classroom Assessment Techniques*, Angelo and Cross describe 50 different CATs, so an exploration of these is well worth the effort. CATs not only give you useful information about learning, but research has shown how they can have positive instructional benefits, such as increasing students' perceptions of the quality of their learning and increasing levels of activity by stimulating class participation. One of the most important elements of good teaching is feedback, and CATs can help in this. Of course, it is essential you give your students feedback on the outcomes of these exercises too! Remember that one of our key principles in the Statement was that reliable and valid assessment of learning and giving helpful feedback on students work is a distinguishing characteristic of good teaching.

Evaluating learning in these ways will yield a rich variety of information. But it may be lacking in one important respect – it may not indicate ways in which you can improve. To find this out, you have to ask your students (and maybe your colleagues too). There are a number of ways you can do this that range from a frank discussion with one student or group to sophisticated student-rating systems.

Evaluating your teaching

As we have seen in Figure 10.2, questionnaires are only one way you can gather information about your teaching. Depending on what you wish to evaluate and why, we think that you will find it necessary to use more than one technique. For example, several of our colleagues use focus groups in which issues are explored in depth with small groups. They also use the evaluation discussion technique from time to time and arrange to visit each others' classes for observation and feedback. Increasingly, some are using e-mailed questions and feedback from students as a means of evaluation too.

Examples of evaluation tools are given in various parts of this book, for example in chapters 3 and 4. We also suggest that, if you do not have ready access to an evaluation service on your campus, you should consult one of the many books on the subject. Centra gives examples of several questionnaires in his book, and we think you will find these helpful.

If you decide to use questionnaires, we suggest you give careful consideration to the following:

● That the evaluation questions asked of students accurately reflect the learning and teaching that they have experienced.
● That students are able to answer questions based on their direct experience of teaching (for example, a first-year student will generally not be in a position to judge whether a teacher's subject knowledge is up to date, whereas a graduate student or colleague may well be able to make such a judgement).
● That when an individual is being evaluated for summative purposes, only responses to questions about matters that the individual can reasonably be held accountable for are used and reported on.

In recent years, there has been considerable innovation in university teaching, and methods such as problem-based learning, resource-based learning and computer-assisted instruction have evolved. Teams of teachers are more commonly responsible for the development and implementation of teaching. Moreover, there has been an expansion of teaching at graduate level where individual supervision of research projects is common. These different approaches to teaching demand different approaches to evaluation, and the points we have made above apply to these as well. If you find yourself teaching in one or more of these situations, we think you need to be fully aware of the general issues presented here and should also seek help and guidance from more specialized literature (some of which is commented on in the Guided Reading section) or from staff in your teaching unit.

Recommendations for using evaluations for developmental purposes (formative evaluation)

The outcomes of all your evaluations should be included in your teaching portfolio. An important part of any portfolio is a section in which you complete a critical self-review, or 'reflection', of your teaching. We say more about this below.

As well as having a plan of action, our other major recommendation is to discuss the outcomes of an evaluation with someone, perhaps an adviser or consultant on teaching, or a trusted colleague or mentor. In addition, a frank discussion with your students will yield two positive benefits. First, it gives them feedback on the outcomes of the evaluation and about your plan to act on the information they have given you. Secondly, you will be able to clarify some areas and seek suggestions from them for changes.

Recommendations for using evaluations for administrative purposes (summative evaluation)

In this rather longer part, we summarize some of the current ideas in research about using evaluations for administrative purposes such as promotion or tenure. Because you will find that there is ongoing debate and dispute about some of these recommendations, we have provided some references so that you can review the findings and the more detailed reasoning behind them.

- It is more appropriate to document and describe your achievements in teaching, and to relate these to your specified duties and expectations than it is to pursue some quantitative criterion, such as a 'magic number' derived from evaluative data (eg a score of six on a seven-point scale). Several sources of valid evaluative information are preferred over any single source. For example, a portfolio approach which combines peer evaluation, student evaluation and appropriate evidence from other sources is recommended (see Magin, 1998).
- If questionnaires are used, short-rating forms with fewer global items are recommended rather than forms that contain a large number of heterogeneous items. Examples of global items should relate to a teacher's responsibilities ('the stated aims were achieved', 'accessible to students' or 'feedback provided promptly') or an overall rating of effective-

ness, rather than to stylistic questions ('I liked the presentation techniques' or 'enthusiastic') (see Scriven, 1981; Magin, 1998).

- Whatever kinds of statistical scores are used in a report on teaching, only broad categories of final judgement should be made (such as 'outstanding', 'adequate', and 'unacceptable'; or 'promote' and 'do not promote') (see McKeachie, 1997).

- The circumstances under which evaluations are collected and analysed should be appropriate and rigorously applied. Standardized procedures should be used for legal and ethical reasons (see d'Apollonia and Abrami, 1997).

- Evaluations should be collected before final examinations (see d'Apollonia and Abrami, 1997).

- You should avoid comparing teachers by using numerical means or medians. Comparisons of ratings from different groups, even within a specific discipline, is a very dubious exercise because of the myriad of variables, such as between-class differences among students; teachers' genders; different goals, learning and teaching methods and assessment arrangements; different course content; and varying degrees of course difficulty. Just as important as the mean or median is the spread of scores – the standard deviation – which raises issues about how much variation in perception of experience exists within groups. Comparisons are not necessary for personnel decision making. What *is* necessary is evidence to allocate the teacher to one of two or three broad categories, such as 'promote' or 'do not promote', and this can be achieved by looking at the overall distribution of student ratings on key questions such as teacher effectiveness. However, this allocation of categories should not just be based on student evaluation, but done by considering other sources of evidence, such as peer evaluation and portfolios. Moreover, an institution that uses comparisons based on means condemns, by definition, half of its teachers, no matter how excellent they are, to always being below average – hardly a positive strategy to motivate people! (see McKeachie, 1997).

A key observation made in McKeachie's paper (p 1218) can be a guiding principle in using student evaluations for summative purposes. He declares: '... the basic problem is not with the ratings but rather with the lack of sophistication of those using them for personnel purposes'.

BRINGING IT ALL TOGETHER: A FRAMEWORK FOR THE EVALUATION OF YOUR TEACHING

By now, you will be aware of the complexity of evaluation, and we hope that the following framework will help you think about the ways in which you evaluate your teaching and also other aspects of your academic work. For example, our focus is on the documentation necessary to assist in a summative evaluation, but this focus can incorporate both the formative evaluation of teaching and of learning because the process of thoughtful documentation is likely to stimulate careful reflection about your practices which may, in turn, lead to improvements.

In a major publication on evaluation, *Scholarship Assessed: Evaluation of the Professoriate*, a broad framework is proposed that is intended to apply to all forms of academic scholarship, including teaching. Applied to teaching and learning, the main elements of the framework are:

● establishing standards of teaching as scholarly work;
● documenting teaching;
● ensuring a trustworthy system of evaluation.

Establishing standards

Teaching evaluation can be guided by the following qualitative standards. You will recognize most of these, as they reflect the qualities of good teaching that we keep reminding you about!

1. Clear goals;
2. Adequate preparation;
3. Appropriate methods;
4. Significant results;
5. Effective presentation;
6. Reflective critique.

1. Clear Goals

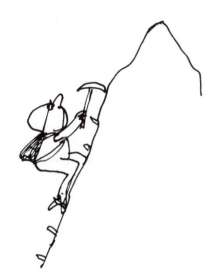

If you look again at our Statement of Educational Principles, you will note that 'clear goals' was identified as one element of the organization of effective teaching identified by research. Having clear, realistic and achievable goals is an indicator of an understanding of the nature of good teaching and learning, but having clear goals is of little value if they cannot realistically be met. Consider the following:

● Have you stated the goals of your teaching clearly, including learning outcomes?
● Have you defined goals that are clear, realistic and achievable?

2. Adequate preparation

Preparation involves the identification and bringing together of resources and materials to support teaching. The following questions may help you here:

● Do you demonstrate an understanding of existing scholarship in your field?
● Do you bring the necessary skills and understanding about learning and teaching to your work as a teacher?
● Do you obtain and organize the resources necessary to achieve your goals?

3. Appropriate methods

Methods and procedures appropriate to the goals and your context have to be chosen, applied effectively, and modified and adapted as teaching proceeds. Methods make a great difference in teaching, from the methods used to organize and present a syllabus, to learning and teaching methods, and assessment arrangements. The following questions are relevant here:

- Do you use methods appropriate to the goals?
- Do you apply these methods effectively?
- Do you modify your methods in response to changing circumstances and feedback?

4. Significant results

Teaching will ultimately be judged by its results as well as by the quality and integrity of its processes. We often ask about learning outcomes in our questionnaires to students: whether the teacher stimulated their interest, whether their ability to work independently has been increased, and the extent of their understanding. The significance of the outcomes of teaching might be judged by asking yourself questions like:

- Did your students achieve your stated goals?
- Does your scholarship in teaching make a difference to your students and to your field of work?
- Does your work open up new areas for development or enquiry?

5. Effective presentation

The importance of presentation in teaching, whether it is presentation in a traditional lecture setting or the presentation of learning materials using electronic technology, is of major significance. Teaching scholarship should lead to presentations to colleagues through publications and conferences as well as presentations to students. The following questions are relevant here:

- Do you use presentation methods appropriate to your goals and teaching context?
- Do you use appropriate forums to present your teaching scholarship?
- Do you present with appropriate clarity and integrity?

6. Reflective critique

The final standard involves a teacher continuing to learn about his or her work by actively seeking out feedback from others so that the whole process of teaching can be monitored and improved. A critical reflection about your teaching should be included here. Reflection can be evaluated by asking these questions:

● Do you regularly evaluate your own work?
● Do you bring to this evaluation a broad range of evidence?
● Do you critically integrate evaluation, reflect on it and use it to improve the quality of your teaching?

Documenting teaching: the teaching portfolio

The second part of the framework is documenting your teaching. The purpose of documentation is to provide the evidence that can be used to judge the extent to which the standards have been achieved. Our purpose here is to focus on how you might record your academic achievements. A valuable tool in working towards this purpose is the 'teaching portfolio', or teaching dossier.

Your portfolio might have three main parts:

1. First, should come a statement of responsibilities, defining what you are required to do or hope to accomplish. This is the basis against which your work will be judged.
2. Second, there should be a statement of your philosophy of teaching and learning, preferably in relation to your institution's goals and plans. This might also include a very brief biographical note outlining the breadth and depth of your scholarly work as a teacher.
3. The third part of your portfolio will be the summarized evidence of your achievements and effectiveness as a teacher. Figure 10.3 gives an extensive list of items that might be appropriate. This summarized evidence can be organized using the standards

described above: clear goals, adequate preparation, appropriate methods, significant results, effective presentation and reflective critique.

There are several reasons why we advocate the preparation and maintenance of a portfolio. These reasons are:

- **Self-evaluation.** The summary you prepare provides an invaluable record of your teaching, which can assist you to reflect on your teaching over a particular period (say, a semester or a year) and to make improvements should these be necessary.
- **Evidence for new appointments, tenure, annual review or promotion.** Institutional appointments and promotions committees increasingly demand evidence of teaching accomplishments to assist them in their decision making. This reflects a worldwide emphasis on better-quality teaching, so it is very wise to have maintained a portfolio for at least the past two or three years. A portfolio will also be very useful in your annual review.
- **Evidence in cases where your teaching is challenged.** In these days of increasing accountability and staff appraisal, there may be occasions upon which the quality of your work is challenged. Documentary evidence maintained by you in your portfolio may prove invaluable in defending your case.
- **Fostering the discussion and reviewing of teaching.** Keeping a portfolio and encouraging others to do so will help to create an environment in which the discussion of teaching becomes the norm rather than an unusual practice in your department.

Do remember that a teaching portfolio is a *summary* of your major teaching activities and accomplishments; it is an important adjunct to your curriculum vitae (CV). It should not include all the material listed in Figure 10.3. Accordingly, you should initially be comprehensive in your collection of information for your portfolio, then summarize the material when it is to be used for some external audience.

FIGURE 10.3   *POSSIBLE CONTENT FOR A TEACHING PORTFOLIO (AFTER SHORE ET AL, 1986)*

The products of good teaching

1. Students' scores on teacher-made or standardized tests, possibly before and after a course has been taken as evidence of learning.
2. Student laboratory workbooks and other kinds of workbooks or logs.
3. Student essays, creative work and project or fieldwork reports.
4. Publications by students on course-related work.
5. A record of your students who select and succeed in advanced courses of study in the field.
6. A record of your students who elect another course with you.
7. Evidence of effective supervision of honours, master's or PhD theses.
8. Setting up or running a successful internship or staff development programme.
9. Documentary evidence of the effect of courses on student career choice.
10. Documentary evidence of your help given to students in securing employment.
11. Evidence of help given to colleagues on teaching improvement.

Materials from oneself: descriptive material on current and recent teaching responsibilities and practices

1. List of course titles and numbers, unit values or credits, enrolment statistics with brief elaboration.
2. List of course materials prepared for students.
3. Information on your availability to students.
4. Report on the identification of student difficulties and encouragement of student participation in courses or programmes.
5. Description of how materials and resources were used in teaching (eg libraries, Internet, etc).
6. Steps taken to emphasize the interrelatedness and relevance of different kinds of learning.

Description of steps taken to evaluate and improve one's teaching

1. Maintaining a record of the changes resulting from self-evaluation.
2. Reading journals on improving teaching and attempting to implement acquired ideas.
3. Reviewing new teaching materials for possible application.
4. Exchanging course materials with a colleague from another institution.
5. Conducting research on one's own teaching or course.
6. Becoming involved in an association or society concerned with the improvement of teaching and learning.
7. Attempting teaching innovations and evaluating their effectiveness.
8. Using general support services such as the Education Resources Information Centre (ERIC) in improving one's teaching.
9. Participating in seminars, workshops and professional meetings intended to improve teaching.
10 Participating in course or curriculum reviews.
11. Pursuing a line of research that contributes directly to teaching.
12. Preparing a textbook or other teaching materials.
13. Editing or contributing to a professional journal on teaching one's subject.

Information from others

Students

1. Student-course and teaching-evaluation data that suggest improvements or produce an overall rating of effectiveness or satisfaction.
2. Written comments from a student committee to evaluate courses and provide feedback.
3. Unstructured (and possibly unsolicited) written evaluations by students, including written comments on exams and letters received after a course has been completed.

4. Documented reports of satisfaction with out-of-class contacts.
5. Interview data collected from students after completion of a course.
6. Honours received from students, such as being elected 'teacher of the year'.

Colleagues

1. Statements from colleagues who have observed teaching either as members of a teaching team or as independent observers of a particular course, or who teach other sections of the same course.
2. Written comments from those who teach courses for which a particular course is a prerequisite.
3. Evaluation of contributions to course development and improvement.
4. Statements from colleagues from other institutions on such matters as how well students have been prepared for graduate studies.
5. Honours or recognition such as a distinguished teacher award or election to a committee on teaching.
6. Requests for advice or acknowledgment of advice received by a committee on teaching or similar body.

Other sources

1. Statements about teaching achievements from administrators at one's own institution or from other institutions.
2. Alumni ratings or other graduate feedback.
3. Comments from parents of students.
4. Reports from employers of students (eg in a work-study or cooperative programme).
5. Invitations to teach for outside agencies.
6. Invitations to contribute to the teaching literature.
7. Other kinds of invitations based on one's reputation as a teacher (for example, a media interview on a successful teaching innovation).

Comments on the contents of a portfolio: Figure 10.3

To give you an insight into exactly what a portfolio may contain, we have obtained permission from Professor Chris Knapper of Queen's University, an author of the original work that defined portfolios in Canada, to reproduce (with some minor changes) the list of items that might be included in a teaching portfolio. The list is shown in Figure 10.3. This list is very comprehensive, but there is no suggestion that all items should be included in your portfolio – you should be very selective when relating the items to your particular responsibilities and needs and, as we suggested earlier, you could structure it according to the framework we have provided.

Creating, assembling and using your portfolio

The most important things to remember are: keep evidence of your teaching activities – file away copies of relevant materials, letters received, articles published, evaluations conducted, and so on – and remember that your portfolio is a *summary*. This evidence is the basis from which your portfolio is constructed and the source from which any statements you make in your portfolio can be verified. We suggest that your portfolio might end up being about six to twelve pages long.

To compile your portfolio we recommend the following steps:

1. Clarify the purposes to which the portfolio will be put and choose appropriate criteria to describe and evaluate your teaching.
2. Keep files of back-up material to follow the structure used in the portfolio. Remember, these materials are not part of the portfolio, but are evidence if required.
3. Prepare brief statements of explanation against each of the criteria selected. You should also add your own brief evaluation of the item and the steps you have taken to modify your teaching in light of (say) feed-

back received. For example, in describing your approach to the assessment of student learning, you might refer to an innovative procedure that revealed students' misconceptions, and then go on to say how you handled these misconceptions in subsequent teaching. Similarly, rather than simply presenting the results of student evaluations, you should also say how you have used the evaluations to change or improve your teaching.

4.   Incorporate the portfolio into your CV.

5.   Finally, remember to constantly review your portfolio and keep it up to date. It is surprising how easy it is to forget the diverse teaching activities we undertake and the feedback we receive. Remember too that your portfolio is an important tool for learning about your teaching. Use it for this purpose also!

Ensuring a trustworthy system of evaluation

The final part of the framework for an evaluation system is ensuring that the system in place is 'trustworthy'. We cannot go into much detail about this here, but the following quotation from *Scholarship Assessed* summarizes what we have in mind:

> ... successful evaluation would be a process with clear goals for institutional and individual performance and adequate preparation for evaluators and candidates. Appropriate methods would be used and significant results would advance the institution and individual towards their goals. The process would be effectively presented and discussed as openly as possible in public forums. Finally, reflective critique would keep evaluation flexible and open to improvement over time. (p.51)

We do not expect that you will be able to change your institution's policies and practices overnight. But, by talking about the characteristics of good evaluation with the right people, you will have an influence upon bringing about useful improvements for the advancement of learning and teaching.

GUIDED READING

There is a wealth of material on evaluation and you may care to check your library's holdings for recent books and guides. A good overview of evaluation – the issues, methods, and resources – is John Centra's *Reflective Faculty Evaluation* (Jossey-Bass, San Franciso, 1993). This book also explores evaluating research and service, and so complements *Scholarship Assessed*, the details of which are noted below.

On portfolios, the most straightforward advice is contained in the original Canadian work on this subject by B Shore, S Foster, C Knapper, G Nadeau, N Neill and V Sim called *The Teaching Dossier: Guide to its preparation and use* (Canadian Association of University Teachers, 1986). Another useful introduction to portfolios, which also considers their relationship to scholarship, is *The Teaching Portfolio: Capturing the scholarship of teaching* by R Edgerton, P Hutchings and K Quinlan (American Association for Higher Education, Washington DC, 1991).

If you are concerned with evaluating materials and educational technologies, we suggest Martin Tessmer's *Planning and Conducting Formative Evaluations* (Kogan Page, London, 1993). This book is an interesting mixture of useful guidance on planning evaluations, evaluating materials, and the whole notion of formative evaluation. James Hartley's *Designing Instructional Text* (Kogan Page, London, 1994) is also helpful on evaluating materials.

Books and articles referred to in this chapter

Angelo, T A and Cross, K P (1993) *Classroom Assessment Technique*, 2nd Edn, Jossey-Bass, San Francisco.

d'Apollonia, S and Abrami, P C (1997) 'Navigating Student Ratings of Instruction', *American Psychologist*, November, pp 1198–1208.

Glassick, Charles E *et al* (1997) *Scholarship Assessed, Evaluation of the Professoriate*, Jossey-Bass, San Francisco.

McKeachie, W J (1997) 'Student Ratings, The Validity of Use', *American Psychologist*, November, pp 1218–1225.

Magin, Doug (1998) 'Rewarding good teaching: A matter of demonstrated proficiency or documented achievement?', *The International Journal of Academic Development*, 3, 2, pp 124–135.

Scriven, M (1981) 'Summative teacher evaluation', in J Millman (ed) *Handbook of Teacher Evaluation*, pp 244–271, Sage, Beverly Hills.

Index